The Ghosts
In Shakespeare

The Ghosts In Shakespeare

A Study of the Occultism in the
Shakespeare Plays

By

L. W. ROGERS

The Theosophical Press
Wheaton, Illinois

AUTHOR'S NOTE

In six of the Shakespeare plays occult phenomena constitute so important a part of them
that they are presented under the titles of those
dramas, while phenomena which are of a more
incidental character are grouped under the divisions of dreams, ceremonial magic, etc.

PREFACE

If the value of literature depends upon the impression it makes upon the human race, there is nothing except the various scriptures of the world that rank with the Shakespeare plays. Most things that are written are soon forgotten. Thousands of books come weekly from the presses. They are read by comparatively few and pass to oblivion unknown to the millions. Occasionally a novel or a drama does attain considerable fame and wide circulation. It is the sensation of the day but the commotion it causes soon subsides and in a few years it is heard of no more. Not many books live a decade. Those that are known to a second generation are exceedingly rare.

With the ephemeral character of literature in mind it is impressive to reflect that the Shakespeare plays are more than three centuries old and are more popular today than in the past. They have been translated into all languages and they are probably more widely read and more frequently quoted than anything else in print. The philosophy, the poetry, the artistry of the Shakespeare plays has, for generations, been the subject of almost universal praise, and again and again the critics have pronounced the author the greatest genius of the race. It becomes a matter of interest to know what so great a soul thinks upon any subject. When he put ghosts and fairies in the plays did he do it to secure dramatic and artistic effects or did he intend them to be a faithful interpretation of the truths of nature? It is for the purpose of arriving at the real intention of the great dramatist that the following pages are written.

A consideration of the occultism to be found in the Shakespeare plays need not involve the question of their authorship. It does not appear to be very important whether Shakespeare or Bacon wrote them. The thing that *is* important is that we now possess them and that they contain a world of wisdom for the student of human nature. The really great mind is not concerned with posthumous fame. It is interested only in doing its work for the race. Why should we waste time quarrelling over a matter that would not interest the person who wrote the plays? Regardless of the authorship of these profound and wonderful delineations of human nature, we have them for our instruction and entertainment. We can study them for their intrinsic value—especially for the great heart lessons they teach

—and reflect that such gems from any other pen would have like worth.

A thought might be offered here on the moral soundness of the plays. There are those who have placed emphasis on what they call the "vile language" that is occasionally encountered in the original. That is an incident. It was the common language of the day and is characteristic of those times. The same indictment can be laid against other literature of that, and earlier periods, including the Bible. Styles of expression change with the age. What is conventionally proper now may be considered coarse three centuries hence. The plays would undoubtedly be better if some of the lines had not been written, but as a whole they present the highest ideals. Purity is determined by fundamental human relationships, rather than by the words in which the thought about them is recorded, and the sound morality taught in the plays constitutes one of their chief virtues. Where in all literature shall we find more inspiring examples of womanly grace and purity than in such characters as Marina in *Pericles*, Desdemona in *Othello*, or Isabella in *Measure for Measure?* We rightly judge an author by the conceptions he deliberately puts in print. If the creation of lofty characters, of men of fine conduct and noble life, of women of purity and tenderness, of all the highest ideals known to the human mind be outward evidence of an author's inner being then these plays testify that the mind that conceived them was one of the noblest of our race.

L. W. R.

CONTENTS

HAMLET, PRINCE OF DENMARK

It is an amusing fact that materialists often quote the phrase, "the undiscovered country from whose bourn no traveler returns," as some sort of evidence that the author of *Hamlet* was a materialist! It ought to be clear even to the casual reader that, since this expression occurs in the soliloquy of Hamlet, it no more represents the belief of the author than Othello's murderous language proves that Shakespeare thought that wives unjustly suspected of wrongdoing should be sentenced to death by jealous husbands. Why should we presume Hamlet to represent the author's beliefs more than Richard or Iago or even Caliban?

Moreover, it does not indicate materialistic philosophy on Hamlet's part. There is certainly nothing remarkable in the fact that he should have employed that phrase. It is not at all inconsistent with his recent conversation with one who *did* return from that "undiscovered country," nor does it indicate any doubt in Hamlet's mind that there is conscious existence after bodily death.

> For in that sleep of death what dreams may
> come,
> When we have shuffled off this mortal coil,
> Must give us pause.

It is not doubt of after-life that troubles him but doubt about what the conditions of that existence may be. In the very wording of the phrase in question he shows that he is no materialist. He asserts the existence of the "country," and employs the phrase merely to show that we have little real knowledge of it.

> But that the dread of something after death,
> The undiscover'd country from whose bourn
> No traveler returns, puzzles the will,
> And makes us rather bear those ills we have
> Than fly to others that we know not of?

As the language runs "undiscovered country" is equivalent to unexplored country. If "discovery" is used in the limited sense of finding we would be deprived of the very subject of our discussion, for unless a country has been found we could not know of it at all. Some kind of a state of existence after physical death he takes for granted and his whole trouble is his uncertainty whether it is better or worse than this state of existence.

Little was then known of such distant countries as India and China. In the same sense they were undiscovered—that is, unexplored. A very few travelers went and returned with accounts of their observations. Explorations into the state of superphysical consciousness were evidently unknown to Hamlet and hence the remark "the undiscovered country from whose bourn no traveler returns." It is a poetic reference to death-land in the terms of a life journey.

The remarkable materialism of our times, that determinedly seeks to explain all phenomena in purely physical terms, nowhere does greater violence to reason than in the attempt to make it appear that the ghost of Hamlet's father is merely intended to be "objectification of the mental condition of Hamlet." It is argued that what he sees, or thinks he sees, is identical with his state of mind at the moment; that Hamlet suspects his uncle of the murder and that when the ghost says, "The serpent that did sting thy father's life now wears his crown," Hamlet exclaims, "O my prophetic soul! My uncle!" and then the ghost goes on to fuller confirmation, all of which is in harmony with Hamlet's preconceived opinions. Thus runs the argument.

That Hamlet was not a materialist is apparent from his ready acceptance of the story of his three friends, that they had seen his father's ghost. He does not express the slightest doubt about the reality of their experience as Horatio had done when he first heard the story, before he had himself seen the ghost. On the contrary, Hamlet expresses no incredulity at all but only wonder, and after the departure of his friends he speculates upon the meaning of it all, and longs for the coming of the night, with its possibility of bringing the ghost again.

The materialistic theory falls to the ground the moment the text is closely scrutinized. *Hamlet is not the discoverer of the ghost.* Bernardo and Marcellus have seen the ghost twice and have reported it to Horatio, who scoffs at the story as a fantasy. So Marcellus brings him along, when the sentinels are changed at midnight, with the hope that "he may approve our eyes and speak to it." Horatio continues to scoff and replies, "Tush, tush, 'twill not appear." But it does soon appear again and as the ghost moves away Bernardo exclaims:

> How now, Horatio! you tremble and look pale:
> Is not this something more than fantasy?
> What think you on't?

To which Horatio solemnly replies:

> Before my God, I might not this believe
> Without the sensible and true avouch
> Of mine own eyes.

That was the third night on which the ghost had appeared. Hamlet did not see it until the following night. Horatio, urged by his two companions, had spoken to the ghost the third night of its appearance but got no reply. The three soldiers fell to discussing the exciting incident and sought some possible explanation for the visit of the ghost. They exchanged views and agreed that the ghost's appearance was in connection with the threatening attitude of Norway and the preparation for war then going on in Denmark. None of them have a thought that the king was murdered. The fact that he was poisoned, and by his own brother, was the message the ghost conveyed to Hamlet, when he broke away from Horatio and Marcellus and followed the apparition. With all these facts before us the attempt to explain away the ghost as an externalization of Hamlet's mental state is obviously absurd.

Horatio cautiously leads up to the startling announcement of the ghost by saying that he had come to Denmark to see the King's funeral, and thus set Hamlet to talking about his father. The dialogue proceeds:

Horatio:

My lord, I think I saw him yesternight.

Hamlet:
    Saw who?
Horatio:
    My lord, the king your father.
Hamlet:
    The king, my father!
Horatio:
    Season your admiration for a while
    With an attent ear, till I may deliver,
    Upon the witness of these gentlemen,
    This marvel to you.
Hamlet:
    For God's love, let me hear.
Horatio:
    Two nights together had these gentlemen,
    Marcellus and Bernardo, on their watch,
    In the dead vast and middle of the night,
    Been thus encounter'd. A figure like your father,
    Armed at point exactly, cap-a-pe,
    Appears before them, and with solemn march
    Goes slow and stately by them: thrice he walk'd
    By their oppress'd and fear-surprised eyes,
    Within his truncheon's length; whilst they, dis-
        till'd
    Almost to jelly with the act of fear,
    Stand dumb, and speak not to him. This to me
    In dreadful secrecy impart they did;
    And I with them the third night kept the watch:
    Where, as they had deliver'd, both in time,
    Form of the thing, each word made true and good,
    The apparition comes: I knew your father;
    These hands are not more like.
Hamlet:
    But where was this?
Marcellus:
    My lord, upon the platform where we watch'd.

After Horatio, Marcellus and Bernardo leave
him Hamlet says:

    My father's spirit in arms! all is not well;

> I doubt some foul play: would the night were
>   come!

The ghost in *Hamlet* is very clearly meant to
be a literal return of the dead king and it is
quite impossible to dispose of it by any theory
of hallucination or by an assumption that it is
a mere dramatic portrayal of the state of mind
of any of the characters who see it. Horatio is
a man of balanced judgment and education.
He has been a fellow student with Prince Hamlet
at Wittenberg. He hears the story of the ghost
from Marcellus with incredulity and insists that
the two officers are the victims of their imag-
inations. Marcellus says to his brother officer,
Bernardo,

> Horatio says 'tis but our fantasy,
> And will not let belief take hold of him
> Touching this dreaded sight, twice seen of us.

Horatio was evidently not the sort of man who
accepts easily the tales of the credulous, but a
hard-headed skeptic, who, before he had himself
seen the ghost, believed that his friends were
deceiving themselves. Clearly he was not in
the frame of mind to lightly credit an imaginary
story or to be himself misled by anything which
he might see.

The testimony of those who have investigated
psychic phenomena is uniformly to the effect that

the popular idea of ghosts, as something arrayed in filmy white drapery, is not true to the facts. Such presentation on the stage is common but there is nothing in the Shakespeare text to authorize it. It is nearer the facts to say that the phantom appears as he was commonly dressed during life and looks not like a "ghost" at all, but like his familiar, living self. A lady whose husband had passed on, some months previously, asked an investigator of psychic phenomena to explain what seemed to her the remarkable fact that when she saw the apparition of her dead husband he "did not look like a ghost, but was dressed as usual, even to the straw hat he had recently worn"—a description that went far toward convincing the investigator of the genuineness of her experience. And so it is in the case of the returned dead king:

Marcellus:
    Is it not like the king?
Horatio:
    As thou art to thyself:
    Such was the very armour he had on
    When he the ambitious Norway combated;
    So frown'd he once, when, in an angry parle,
    He smote the sledded Polacks on the ice.
    'Tis strange.

Again in the final appearance of the ghost, during Hamlet's arraignment of his mother in

Act III, in expressing his surprise that the queen does not see the ghost, Hamlet says:

My father, in his habit as he lived;

The fact that the queen did not see the ghost has sometimes been cited as evidence that it was only a product of Hamlet's overwrought mind; but even if that were true it could not invalidate the fact that the ghost on its previous visits was real enough. The impossibility of disposing of the experiences of Marcellus, Bernardo and Horatio on the theory of hallucination has already been discussed. The genuineness of that experience, which converted a skeptic and scoffer, stands unimpaired, whatever be the explanation of the incident in Act III. The reasonable explanation, however, is that some of us are much less sensitive than others and it seems probable that the queen was one of those who would have difficulty in seeing an apparition which might be quite visible to others. The fact that one person is sensitive to colors so high in the spectrum that they are invisible to others, is well known, while the camera registers vibrations higher than those to which the most sensitive retina can respond.

Those who would find for the introduction of such phenomena as materialization in these plays some explanation that is consistent with the idea that "only children and old women believe in ghosts" will assuredly have trouble enough in any attempt to erase the occultism from *Hamlet* and have anything left. It is not incidental. It holds the very center of the stage. The communication between Hamlet and the ghost is by no means trivial or casual. The whole future of the tragedy turns upon this pivotal point. Hamlet shapes his program by the information thus received. Through this materialization he comes into possession of the proof that his father was murdered and learns by whom and in what treacherous and cowardly manner it was accomplished. Hamlet applies physical tests to this psychical information and, thus getting full confirmation, no shadow of doubt remains.

Now, why should the great dramatist introduce the ghost unless it is his desire to give us a glimpse of what lies beyond the range of the physical senses—to present all the actors vitally concerned in the drama, whether belonging to the physical realm or not, and to portray their passions and emotions as they are, with their intimate connection with, and possible influence upon, the visible world? The truth of nature

here presented is that the death of the physical
body does not change a man—that he is the
same individual, mentally and morally, after
bodily death as before it, with the same kind of
thoughts and emotions that he had during physical life. The dead king is represented as having
just such emotions as he would have had if, instead of having been murdered, he had been
banished and imprisoned but had escaped and
returned. He desires revenge. He has been deprived of his kingdom and his life, and his murderer has married his widow. He is enraged and
takes the same course that a living man, under
the same circumstances, would take. He incites
Hamlet to avenge him and when Hamlet is too
slow in coming to the point (Act III, Scene IV)
the dead king appears again to urge him on:

Ghost:
> Do not forget: this visitation
> Is but to whet thy almost blunted purpose.

It was certainly not necessary to invent a
ghost in order to acquaint Hamlet with the
identity of his father's murderer. It could easily have been done by some secreted person who
observed 'the uncle's act—after the method of
the more materialistic dramatists who, with more
regard to startling effects than to exact repre-

sentations of nature, are never at a loss for means to lay bare a secret, and, if need be, to make uncertain threads meet, to create a few spies out of hand while you wait! If the purpose of this master dramatist was not to give us a picture of human life that reaches beyond the visible, to describe the passions and emotions as surviving the loss of the physical body, then the bringing forward of the ghost violates one of the first principles of dramatic art: the introduction of the superfluous. Unless the purpose is akin to that indicated the appearance of the ghost is a clumsy, absurd blunder; and so free are the Shakespeare plays from artistic flaws that when anything is found in them that does not play a necessary part in the whole—does not contribute a ray of light toward the complete illumination of the subject under consideration— the critics conclude it is one of the interpolations that have crept in since the plays left the author's hands. The only logical inference to be drawn is that all the varied occultism to be found in the plays is there for a purpose—the very sane purpose of giving us a full and faithful picture of things as they really are and not as those who see only with physical eyes imagine them to be.

MACBETH

After *Hamlet, Macbeth* is apparently the most popular of the tragedies and it presents an attractive array of occult phenomena. As in the former tragedy there is nothing incidental about its occultism. It runs consistently throughout the play. The curtain rises to it and it holds a most conspicuous position to the very end, for it is only in the last scene of the final act that the exact fulfillment of the witches' prophecies is made clear. These witches and their predictions play a vital part in the drama. They are represented as having knowledge of future events and they give accurate descriptions of what is to occur. All that follows, until the very end, is but the working out in the visible world of events thus forecast.

It will be remembered that it is in the third scene of the first act that Macbeth and Banquo are returning victorious from the battlefield when the witches are encountered and that they hail Macbeth as thane of Cawdor, an honor the king is about to confer upon him and of which

he is entirely ignorant. They couple this information with the prophecy that he is to be king
of Scotland. Before he leaves the spot he learns
that the first part of the prophecy has been
swiftly fulfilled, and he naturally has faith in
the rest of it; and, his mind full of the possibility of attaining the crown, he promptly begins
plotting to that end. Thus is laid the basis for
the whole action of the play.

The old argument of "externalization of inner
conditions" has been invoked to explain the
witches in a way satisfactory to materialistic
interpretation, but it is no more satisfactory
here than it was in *Hamlet*.

The most casual reading of the text will show
the fallacy of that hypothesis. Both Banquo
and Macbeth see and converse with the witches.
If the weird sisters are but an objectification of
what is in Macbeth's mind how could Banquo
participate? Moreover, it is Banquo who first
sees and speaks to the witches, as he and Macbeth enter together, and it is he who calls Macbeth's attention to them. But there are other
reasons why the witches cannot represent the
contents of Macbeth's mind. They make prophecies about the future and these relate to both
of the men before them. When Macbeth chal-

lenges them to speak, the first witch correctly names him thane of Glamis. The second witch hails him as thane of Cawdor (which he at that instant was, although the news of his promotion had not reached him) while the third witch said, "All hail, Macbeth! that shalt be king hereafter!"

Macbeth:
    So foul and fair a day I have not seen.
Banquo:
    How far is't call'd to Forres? What are these
    So wither'd, and so wild in their attire,
    That look not like the inhabitants o' the earth,
    And yet are on't? Live you? or are you aught
    That man may question? You seem to under-
        stand me,
    By each at once her choppy finger laying
    Upon her skinny lips: you should be women,
    And yet your beards forbid me to interpret
    That you are so.
Macbeth:
    Speak, if you can: what are you?
First Witch:
    All hail, Macbeth! hail to thee, thane of Glamis!
Second Witch:
    All hail, Macbeth! hail to thee, thane of Cawdor!
Third Witch:
    All hail, Macbeth, that shalt be king hereafter!
Banquo:
    Good sir, why do you start, and seem to fear
    Things that do sound so fair? I' the name of
        truth,
    Are ye fantastical, or that indeed
    Which outwardly ye show? My noble partner
    You greet with present grace and great prediction
    Of noble having and of royal hope,
    That he seems rapt withal: to me you speak not:

> If you can look into the seeds of time,
> And say which grain will grow and which will not,
> Speak then to me, who neither beg nor fear
> Your favors nor your hate.

First Witch:
> Hail!

Second Witch:
> Hail!

Third Witch:
> Hail!

First Witch:
> Lesser than Macbeth, and greater.

Second Witch:
> Not so happy, yet much happier.

Third Witch:
> Thou shalt get kings, though thou be none:
> So all hail, Macbeth and Banquo!

First Witch:
> Banquo and Macbeth, all hail!

Macbeth:
> Stay, you imperfect speakers, tell me more:
> By Sinel's death I know I'm thane of Glamis;
> But how of Cawdor? the thane of Cawdor lives,
> A prosperous gentleman; and to be king
> Stands not within the prospect of belief,
> No more than to be Cawdor. Say from whence
> You owe this strange intelligence? or why
> Upon this blasted heath you stop our way
> With such prophetic greeting? Speak, I charge
> you.

> > *[Witches vanish.*

Thus did the witches prophesy about the future, and the prophecy proves to be true to the facts as the tragedy unfolds and discloses the future. To the very end of the play they give an accurate forecast of events. Of course the weird sisters would not be represented as

being capable of doing that if they are intended
to reflect the mental processes of Macbeth.

Although the witches vanished at the moment
when Macbeth asked them for an explanation
of why they had addressed him as thane of
Cawdor, he had not long to wait for the solution of the puzzle.   Almost immediately Ross
and Angus enter and the play proceeds:

Angus:
　　We are sent
　　To give thee, from our royal master, thanks;
　　Only to herald thee into his sight,
　　Not pay thee.
Ross:
　　And, for an earnest of a greater honor,
　　He bade me, from him, call thee thane of Cawdor.
　　In which addition, hail, most worthy thane!
　　For it is thine.
Banquo:
　　What, can the devil speak true?
Macbeth:
　　The thane of Cawdor lives: why do you dress me
　　In borrow'd robes?
Angus:
　　Who was the thane lives yet,
　　But under heavy judgment bears that life
　　Which he deserves to lose.   Whether he was com-
　　　　bined
　　With those of Norway, or did line the rebel
　　With hidden help and vantage, or that with both
　　He labor'd· in his country's wreck, I know not;
　　But treasons capital, confess'd and proved,
　　Have overthrown him.
Macbeth [*aside*]:
　　Glamis, and thane of Cawdor:
　　The greatest is behind.

[*To Ross and Angus*]: Thanks for your pains.
[*Aside to Banquo*]: Do you not hope your children
    shall be kings,
When those that gave the thane of Cawdor to
    me
Promised no less to them?

It is impossible to read this dialogue and believe that the witches are intended to represent any subjective states of mind. These were actual entities, conversing with Macbeth and Banquo, and each of them ponders over what both of them heard. Macbeth, having had the proof that the witches foretold the facts about his new title, thane of Cawdor, clearly has high hope that the crown shall also be his, while Banquo looks at the matter from a different viewpoint, and to Macbeth's question above quoted, replies:

Banquo [*aside to Macbeth*]:
    That, trusted home,
    Might yet enkindle you unto the crown,
    Besides the thane of Cawdor. But 'tis strange:
    And oftentimes, to win us to our harm,
    The instruments of darkness tell us truths,
    Win us with honest trifles, to betray's
    In deepest consequence.

In Act IV, Macbeth again visits the witches with the hope of gaining further knowledge about the future. Since first he had met the weird sisters, he had killed the king and caused the assassination of Banquo. Having begun his reign with murder, he seeks to remove all opposition by continued slaughter; but even with the help of his hired assassins, things are not going well with him. He has his paid spies scattered throughout the country, and is thus well informed, but despite espionage and assassination, he feels more and more insecure and resolves to learn whether the witches can give him some indication of what the future holds for him.

If we have in mind just what Macbeth was thinking about, and longing to know, when he sought the witches, the things he saw and heard are more readily understood. He longs, not merely for some token to indicate that he shall hold the throne, despite all the enemies which his bloody course might have raised up against him, but also for some assurance that he is the founder of a dynasty—that sons shall come to inherit the kingdom that he has bought with the heavy price of regicide, and that the house of Macbeth shall live in the future. Prior to Banquo's assassination by Macbeth's orders, the latter broods over the fact that the former's high character is dangerous to Macbeth's security. His fears are well grounded. Banquo had used "a wisdom that doth guide his valor" to

correctly solve the mystery of the murder of the
king, and soliloquizes, in Scene I, Act III:

Banquo:
Thou hast it now: King, Cawdor, Glamis, all,
As the weird women promised, and I fear
Thou play'dst most foully for't.

While waiting for the hired murderers to come,
Macbeth soliloquizes:

Macbeth:
Our fears in Banquo
Stick deep; and in his royalty of nature
Reigns that which would be fear'd: 'tis much he
          dares,
And, to that dauntless temper of his mind,
He hath a wisdom that doth guide his valor
To act in safety. There is none but he
Whose being I do fear: and under him
My genius is rebuked, as it is said
Mark Antony's was by Caesar. He chid the sis-
          ters,
When first they put the name of king upon me,
And bade them speak to him; then prophet-like
They hail'd him father to a line of kings.

His fear of Banquo, however, gives way to
concern about his possession of "a fruitless
crown," and to anxiety about the future. He
is dissatisfied with the prophecy and is determined to challenge fate itself.

Macbeth:
Upon my head they placed a fruitless crown
And put a barren sceptre in my gripe,
Thence to be wrench'd with an unlineal hand,
No son of mine succeeding. If't be so,
For Banquo's issue have I fil'd my mind;

> For them the gracious Duncan have I murder'd;
> Put rancors in the vessel of my peace
> Only for them, and mine eternal jewel,
> Given to the common enemy of man,
> To make them kings, the seed of Banquo kings!
> Rather than so, come fate into the list,
> And champion me to the utterance!

After the assassination of Banquo, he determines to immediately visit the witches again and he says to Lady Macbeth:

> And betimes I will, to the weird sisters:
> More shall they speak, for now I am bent to know,
> By the worst means, the worst. For mine own good
> All causes shall give way: I am in blood
> Stepp'd in so far, that, should I wade no more,
> Returning were as tedious as go o'er.

In this frame of mind, resolved to know the truth whatever it might be, and apprehensive about the succession to the throne, he enters the cavern, Scene I, Act IV.

Macbeth:
> How now, you secret, black, and midnight hags!
> What is't you do?

All:
> A deed without a name.

Macbeth:
> I conjure you, by that which you profess,
> Howe'er you come to know it, answer me:
> Though you untie the winds and let them fight
> Against the churches; though the yesty waves
> Confound and swallow navigation up;
> Though bladed corn be lodged and trees blown down;

> Though castles topple on their warders' heads;
> Though palaces and pyramids do slope
> Their heads to their foundations; though the treasure
> Of nature's germins tumble all together,
> Even till destruction sicken; answer me
> To what I ask you.

After some ceremonial magic by the three witches, the text runs:

Thunder. First Apparition: an armed Head.
Macbeth:
> Tell me, thou unknown power,—

First Witch:
> He knows thy thought:
> Hear his speech, but say thou nought.

First Apparition:
> Macbeth! Macbeth! Macbeth! beware Macduff;
> Beware the thane of Fife. Dismiss me: enough.
> *[Descends.*

Macbeth:
> Whate'er thou art, for thy good caution thanks;
> Thou hast harp'd my fear aright: but one word
> more,—

First Witch:
> He will not be commanded; here's another,
> More potent than the first.
> *Thunder. Second Apparition: a bloody Child.*

Second Apparition:
> Macbeth! Macbeth! Macbeth!

Macbeth:
> Had I three ears, I'd hear thee.

Second Apparition:
> Be bloody, bold and resolute; laugh to scorn
> The power of man, for none of woman born
> Shall harm Macbeth.   *[Descends.*

Macbeth:
> Then live, Macduff: what need I fear of thee?
> But yet I'll make assurance double sure,
> And take a bond of fate: thou shalt not live;

That I may tell pale-hearted fear it lies,
And sleep in spite of thunder.
Thunder. Third Apparition: a Child crowned, with a
*   tree in his hand.*
What is this,
That rises like the issue of a king,
And wears upon his baby-brow the round
And top of sovereignty?
All:
Listen, but speak not to't.
Third Apparition:
Be lion-mettled, proud, and take no care
Who chafes, who frets, or where conspirers are:
Macbeth shall never vanquish'd be until
Great Birnam wood to high Dunsinane hill
Shall come against him.   [*Descends.*
Macbeth:
That will never be:
Who can impress the forest, bid the tree
Unfix his earth-bound root? Sweet bodements!
     good!
Rebellion's head, rise never till the wood
Of Birnam rise, and our high-placed Macbeth
Shall live the lease of nature, pay his breath
To time and mortal custom.

Each one of these prophecies is fulfilled to the
very letter before the tragedy runs its course;
but they are not, in the main, correctly inter-
preted by Macbeth. They seem to him to be
assurances that he is invulnerable and that
his enemies cannot prevail against him.

His confidence in his future is now complete.
He believes a long reign is ahead for him.
This confidence is as great as had been his am-
bition to become king. Had not the witches told

him of his first promotion before it occurred?
Had they not then truly prophesied that he
would be king? Now he was being given, apparently, such unmistakable pledges of future
security that he felt certain he would finally
die a natural death—would "live the lease of
nature." And so, lured on by his misinterpre-
tation of what he had seen and heard, he went
straight forward to his doom, which, to the
smallest particular, fulfilled the prophecy.

Just how Macbeth felt about it is portrayed
in Scene III of Act V, when the reports of the
advance of the English forces had reached him:

Macbeth:
> Bring me no more reports; let them fly all;
> Till Birnam wood remove to Dunsinane
> I cannot taint with fear. What's the boy Mal-
> colm?
> Was he not born of woman? The spirits that
> know
> All mortal consequences have pronounced me
> thus:
> 'Fear not, Macbeth; no man that's born of woman
> Shall e'er have power upon thee.' Then fly,
> false thanes,
> And mingle with the English epicures:
> The mind I sway by and the heart I bear
> Shall never sag with doubt nor shake with fear.
>   *Enter a Servant.*
> The devil damn thee black, thou   cream-faced
> loon!
> Where gott'st thou that goose look?

Servant:
> There is ten thousand—

Macbeth:
> Geese, villain?

Servant:
> Soldiers, sir.

Macbeth:
> Go prick thy face and over-red thy fear,
> Thou lily-liver'd boy. What soldiers, patch?
> Death of thy soul! those linen cheeks of thine
> Are counsellors to fear. What soldiers, whey-
>   face?

Servant:
> The English force, so please you.

Later in the Scene, while talking to the Doctor, Macbeth remarks:

> I will not be afraid of death and bane
> Till Birnam forest come to Dunsinane.

Up to this point Macbeth has perfect confidence in the prophecy of the weird sisters but events are soon to disillusion him.

Scene IV is the country near Birnam wood, and marching soldiers enter led by Malcolm, the son of the murdered king, his uncle Siward, Macduff, Menteith and others:

Siward:
> What wood is this before us?

Menteith:
> The wood of Birnam.

Malcolm:
> Let every soldier hew him down a bough
> And bear't before him: thereby shall we shadow
> The numbers of our host, and make discovery
> Err in report of us.

Soldiers:
> It shall be done.

It is not difficult to imagine the impression which would be made upon an observer at a distance by an advancing army in which each soldier was screened behind a green bough. It was the report of this phenomenon, repeated to Macbeth, that began to unnerve him.

Macbeth:
Thou comest to use thy tongue; thy story quickly.

Messenger:
Gracious my lord,
I should report that which I say I saw,
But know not how to do it.

Macbeth:
Well, say, sir.

Messenger:
As I did stand my watch upon the hill,
I look'd toward Birnam, and anon, methought,
The wood began to move.

Macbeth:
Liar and slave!

Messenger:
Let me endure your wrath if't be not so:
Within this three mile may you see it coming;
I say, a moving grove.

Macbeth.
If thou speak'st false,
Upon the next tree shalt thou hang alive,
Till famine cling thee: if thy speech be sooth,
I care not if thou dost for me as much.
I pull in resolution and begin
To doubt the equivocation of the fiend
That lies like truth: 'Fear not, till Birnam wood
Do come to Dunsinane;' and now a wood
Comes toward Dunsinane. Arm, arm, and out!
If this which he avouches does appear,
There is nor flying hence, nor tarrying here.
I 'gin to be a-weary of the sun,

And wish the estate o' the world were now un-
    done.
Ring the alarum-bell! Blow, wind! come, wrack!
At least we'll die with harness on our back.

When the assaulting column is near the castle,
Malcolm says:

Malcolm:
    Now near enough; your leavy screens throw
        down,
    And show like those you are.

In Scene VII we have the sequel to the two
apparitions Macbeth saw in the cavern of the
witches.   Out on the plain before his castle,
Macbeth fortifies his courage with the words
of the second prophecy:

Macbeth:
    They have tied me to a stake; I cannot fly,
    But bear-like I must fight the course. What's he
    That was not born of woman? Such a one
    Am I to fear, or none.
                    Enter Young Siward.
Young Siward:
    What is thy name?
Macbeth:
    Thou'lt be afraid to hear it.
Young Siward:
    No; though thou call'st thyself a hotter name
    Than any is in hell.
Macbeth:
    My name's Macbeth.
Young Siward:
    The devil himself could not pronounce a title
    More hateful to mine ear.
Macbeth:
    No, nor more fearful.

Young Siward:
    Thou liest, abhorred tyrant; with my sword
    I'll prove the lie you speak'st.
                    [*They fight and Young Siward is slain.*
Macbeth:
    Thou wast born of woman.
    But swords I smile at, weapons laugh to scorn,
    Brandish'd by man that's of a woman born.

But he is soon to learn of his error and to be completely unnerved by the startling information that Macduff did not come within the category of those described by the second apparition, as having no power over Macbeth.

Macbeth:
    Why should I play the Roman fool, and die
    On mine own sword? whiles I see lives, the gashes
    Do better upon them.
                    Enter Macduff.
Macduff:
    Turn, hell-hound, turn!
Macbeth:
    Of all men else I have avoided thee:
    But get thee back; my soul is too much charged
    With blood of thine already.
Macduff:
    I have no words:
    My voice is in my sword, thou bloodier villain
    Than terms can give thee out!   [*They fight.*
Macbeth:
    Thou losest labor:
    As easy mayst thou the intrenchant air
    With thy keen sword impress as make me bleed:
    Let fall thy blade on vulnerable crests;
    I bear a charmed life, which must not yield
    To one of woman born.
Macduff:
    Despair thy charm,

And let the angel whom thou still hast served
Tell thee, Macduff was from his mother's womb
Untimely ripp'd.

Macbeth:
Accursed be that tongue that tells me so,
For it hath cow'd my better part of man:
And be these juggling fiends no more believed,
That palter with us in a double sense;
That keep the word of promise to our ear,
And break it to our hope. I'll not fight with thee.

Macduff:
Then yield thee, coward,
And live to be the show and gaze o' the time:
We'll have thee, as our rarer monsters are,
Painted upon a pole, and underwrit,
'Here may you see the tyrant.'

Macbeth:
I will not yield,
To kiss the ground before young Malcolm's feet,
And to be baited with the rabble's curse.
Though Birnam wood be come to Dunsinane,
And thou opposed, being of no woman born,
Yet I will try the last: before my body
I throw my war-like shield: Lay on, Macduff;
And damn'd be him that first cries "Hold
enough!"

The final item of fulfillment comes at the end
of the play when Macduff re-enters with Macbeth's head. It will be remembered that the
first apparition was merely an armed head
which exclaimed:

Macbeth! Macbeth! Macbeth! beware Macduff;
Beware the thane of Fife.

It is inconceivable that a great dramatist
would construct a play, the entire first part of
which is devoted to prophecies regarding the

chief personage in the drama and the remainder of which is given over to the minutest fulfillment of those prophecies, unless he had a definite purpose to be accomplished by it. It is clearly impossible to call the occultism in *Macbeth* incidental. It is the foundation and the culmination. Some form of occultism is continually impressing itself upon the spectator, and it is all as true to occult principles as the characters are true to human life.

Those who argue that the various apparitions in the Shakespeare plays may be explained as hallucinations are fond of calling attention to the fact that nobody but Macbeth sees the ghost of Banquo at the feast. But that fact is perfectly consistent with the hypothesis that Macbeth really saw what he believed he saw. To the reader who is not familiar with occultism a ghost is a ghost, or it is nothing, and classification of apparitions does not exist for him. But to the student of the occult the case of the return of the dead King of Denmark and the reappearance of Banquo after death represent two distinct classes of phenomena. The first is a materialization while the second is a wraith, and they differ almost as a man differs from his clothing. Ever since Sir William Crookes, the great English chemist, made his famous experiments in the matter of materializations and published in the *Quarterly Journal of Science* the facts that warrant the belief that those who have died from a physical body can sometimes surround themselves with enough dense matter to be seen, to be photographed, to become tangible and to speak, it has been possible to discuss such a subject without being dubbed a sentimentalist or a fool. The whole matter rests upon the most reliable scientific testimony and the public is at last putting prejudice aside and beginning to learn something of the occult facts. But while the fact of materialization is somewhat understood, that of wraiths has had little, if any, scientific attention. Yet occasionally we read in the press of the wraith. The *New York Herald* of July 4, 1908, publishes the following story:

Miss Mary Trimble, of 181 North Seventh street, Roseville, N. J., yesterday declared that her brother, James M. Trimble, who lived at 16 Cedar street, Montclair, appeared to her in an apparition the day after his death and before the news of it had been made known to her or to any members of the family.

Her statement is particularly interesting on

account of an agreement among Mr. Trimble and the members of his immediate family, as well as one with his sister, that in the event of the death of any one of them that one would attempt to communicate with the others.

Mr. Trimble was widely known in Montclair and Newark. He was a lawyer and an Italian scholar.

Miss Trimble, with her brother's wife, Mrs. Lucy Trimble, and the younger of his two sons, Rufus Trimble, was at the Princeton commencement exercises for the graduation of Henry Trimble, the elder son. James M. Trimble had been in ill health for two years, and at the time of his death was in a sanitarium in Verona. The death occurred about eleven o'clock on Monday evening, June 14, but those in charge of the case at the sanitarium withheld the news so that the family's plans for Tuesday night might not be marred. The family did not learn of Mr. Trimble's death until about ten o'clock on Tuesday evening, June 15.

"I was paying particular attention to the Latin oration," Miss Trimble said, "because my brother was a Latin scholar and I was particularly pleased at something I would have to tell him about. I happened to lift my eyes up and saw my brother standing in the doorway on the gallery on the left hand side of Dr. Wilson, the university's president. We were in the gallery on the opposite side.

"My first thought was that he had come down in an automobile because of his interest in the exercises. I grasped the arm of my nephew Rufus, and was just about to say, 'There's your father,' when I realized that it was not my brother's actual body. Instead I just remarked, 'I'll tell you later, I'll tell you later,' and said no more about it at the moment. I did not speak of it again until the exercises were over, when I told the mother and the boys." Miss Trimble said that all through her life she has had "second sight."

There is in existence a great deal of similar evidence regarding wraiths. It is not uncommon to read, or hear, of somebody who has seen the apparition of the dying or of the recently deceased. According to the statement made, Miss Trimble saw her brother's wraith about twenty, or perhaps twenty-one, hours after his death. This appearance so soon after passing out of the physical body and the failure to make any communication are characteristic of the wraith and distinguish it from the materialization. But the usual condition essential to such phenomena relate also to the percipient, if we may use the language of the psychic research experts. The living friend who sees the wraith is either somewhat sensitive, or is ill, or overtaxed, or for some other reason is in an abnormal condition.

Macbeth is naturally much overwrought just preceding, and after, the murder of the king. He represents that unique condition of nerve tension common to temporary clairvoyance. In this state of mind he saw the bloody dagger in the air before him, so real that he tries to grasp it. After he has caused the death of Banquo he sees his victim's wraith. Banquo was on his way to the feast in Macbeth's castle when he was murdered by Macbeth's henchmen. He was hurrying to the castle, with his mind intent upon reaching it, when death overtook him. His wraith appears at the feast, but only Macbeth, with his overwrought nerves, sees it, and his language is fittingly descriptive of wraiths when he says, "Thou hast no speculation in those eyes."

It is most interesting to observe how true to nature and to occult teaching this description of the wraith of Banquo is. Not only the possibility of Macbeth's seeing the wraith but the

probability of its appearing just where and when
it did are faithful to the occult facts. The
thoughts of the dying very naturally have their
after-death influence and aside from occult literature there are frequent reports of the experiences of friends and relatives who have seen
the apparitions of the dead before the news of
the death reached them. But it is not merely to
friends that an apparition may appear. One de-
termining factor seems to be the strong desire of
the dying to be with certain people or at a certain place, whatever the reason might be that
caused the desire. Banquo was late, was riding
hard, and had the whole of his mental energies
upon the problem of arriving at the banquet on
time, when he suddenly met death.

In order that the phenomena of wraiths may
be understood and the naturalness of the description of the appearance of the wraith of Banquo
at the banquet may be fully appreciated it is
necessary to consider the theosophical hypothesis
of the constitution of a human being. The physical body in which we have our waking consciousness and the astral body in which we consciously
exist after bodily death are connected by the
"etheric double," constituting a duplicate, in
etheric matter, of the physical body and occupy-

ing the same space, as air and ether do—the interpenetration of two grades of physical matter of different densities. This etheric double, which is an exact duplicate of the physical body, is nevertheless not a body, for the ego cannot use it as a vehicle of consciousness as both the physical body and the astral body can be used. It is merely the connecting link between them and its function is to convey the life forces to the physical mechanism. Being of physical, though invisible, matter it perishes with the physical body but immediately after bodily death it often plays the role of ghost.

"At what is called death, the etheric double is drawn away from its dense counterpart by the escaping consciousness; the magnetic tie existing betwen them during earth life is snapped asunder, and [sometimes] for some hours the consciousness remains enveloped in this etheric garb. In this it sometimes appears to those with whom it is closely bound up, as a cloudy figure, very dully conscious and speechless—the wraith."

—*The Ancient Wisdom*, p. 56.

"The ego [at the time of bodily death] quickly shakes off the etheric double, which, as we have seen, cannot pass on to the astral plane, and leaves it to disintegrate with its life-long partner. It will sometimes appear immediately after death to friends at no great distance from the corpse, but naturally shows very little consciousness, and will not speak or do anything beyond 'manifesting' itself. It is comparatively easily seen, being physical, and a slight tension of the nervous system will render vision sufficiently acute to discern it."—*Man and His Bodies*, p. 32.

It was this nerve tension that enabled Macbeth to see the wraith of Banquo which, to the others, was invisible. He had just held a brief conference, at the door of the banquet room, with the chief assassin and had learned of Banquo's death, and also of the escape of Fleance who, so far as succession to the throne was concerned, was as dangerous to Macbeth as Banquo, himself. All this naturally wrought him up to the highest pitch, and thus Macbeth, who was naturally inclined to clairvoyance, as the phantom dagger incident shows, was in a condition to perceive what others could not see.

The fruitlessness of this additional murder, the possibility that it might raise up new enemies against him, and the certainty that the witches' prophecy that Banquo would be the father of a line of kings could be made good by the escape of his son, Fleance, would naturally increase the strain on his overwrought nerves and bring him into that condition that would "render vision sufficiently acute" to perceive the wraith.

Returning to the banquet table from the brief conference with the chief murderer, Scene IV, Act III, Macbeth says:

Macbeth:
Now good digestion wait on appetite,
And health on both.

Lennox:
May it please your highness sit?
[*The Ghost of Banquo enters, and sits in Macbeth's place.*]

Macbeth:
Here had we now our country's honor roof'd,
Were the grac'd person of our Banquo present;
Who may I rather challenge for unkindness
Than pity for mischance!

Ross:
His absence, sir,
Lays blame upon his promise. Please 't your highness
To grace us with your royal company.

Macbeth:
The table's full.

Lennox:
Here is a place reserv'd, sir.

Macbeth:
Where?

Lennox:
Here, my good lord. What is't that moves your highness?

Macbeth:
Which of you have done this?

Lords:
What, my good lord?

Macbeth:

>   Thou canst not say I did it: never shake
>   Thy gory locks at me.

Ross:

>   Gentlemen, rise; his highness is not well.

Lady Macbeth:

>   Sit, worthy friends: my lord is often thus,
>   And hath been from his youth: pray you, keep
>   seat;
>   The fit is momentary; upon a thought
>   He will again be well. If much you note him
>   You shall offend him and extend his passion:
>   Feed and regard him not.

Macbeth's exclamations show how deeply he was moved.

Macbeth:

>   Prithee, see there! behold! look! lo! how say you?
>   Why, what care I? If thou canst nod, speak too.
>   If charnel-houses and our graves must send
>   Those that we bury back, our monuments
>   Shall be the maws of kites.

The experienced warrior of many battlefields, who was accustomed to staking his life against odds, trembled with fear before the apparition.

Macbeth:

>   Avaunt! and quit my sight! Let the earth hide
>   thee!
>   Thy bones are marrowless, thy blood is cold;
>   Thou has no speculation in those eyes
>   Which thou dost glare with.

Lady Macbeth:

>   Think of this, good peers,
>   But as a thing of custom: 'tis no other;
>   Only it spoils the pleasure of the time.

Macbeth:

>   What man dare, I dare:

> Approach thou like the rugged Russian bear,
> The arm'd rhinoceros, or the Hyrcan tiger;
> Take any shape but that, and my firm nerves
> Shall never tremble: or be alive again,
> And dare me to the desert with thy sword;
> If trembling I inhabit then, protest me
> The baby of a girl. Hence, horrible shadow!
> Unreal mockery, hence!   [*Ghost vanishes.*
>   Why, so; being gone,
> I am a man again. Pray you, sit still.

There was no "hallucination" about it. He did not look upon a picture painted by that treacherous artist, Fear. Macbeth was not a timid man afraid of shadows, but a veteran warrior of dauntless courage; and to this well-known quality of her husband's character Lady Macbeth promptly appealed in an "aside" to Macbeth:

>   Are you a man?
>
> *Macbeth*:
>   Ay, and a bold one, that dare look on that
>   Which might appall the devil.

Encouraging this attitude of mind Lady Macbeth replies:

>   O proper stuff!
> This is the very painting of your fear;
> This is the air-drawn dagger which, you said,
> Led you to Duncan. O, these flaws and starts,
> Imposters to true fear, would well become
> A woman's story at a winter's fire,
> Authoriz'd by her grandam. Shame itself!
> Why do you make such faces? When all's done,
> You look but on a stool.

But Macbeth saw, and he knew that he saw,

the ghost of his latest victim; and while Lady
Macbeth saw nothing and marvelled to observe
how deeply her husband was moved *he* was as-
tounded to see that she was unmoved, so real
was the murdered Banquo before him. To her
protest that he was throwing the whole assem-
blage into disorder he replies:

> Can such things be,
> And overcome us like a summer's cloud,
> Without our special wonder? You make me
>   strange
> Even to the disposition that I owe,
> When now I think you can behold such
>   sights,
> And keep the natural ruby of your cheeks,
> When mine are blanch'd with fear.

To Macbeth, whose temporary abnormal condition enabled him to see the etheric matter com-
posing the duplicate of the dead man's physical
body, there was no more question of Banquo's
presence than there was of the existence of the
other people in the room. Of course he would
not be conscious of the fact that he could see
what the others could not see. It did not even
occur to him that Lady Macbeth did not see the
wraith. It was as visible to him as the furni-
ture and he expressed his astonishment that she
"can behold such sights" and give no outward
sign of agitation.

The occult side of sleep and dreams is another subject on which a flood of light is thrown in this great tragedy. What, from the occult viewpoint, is the thing we call sleep? It is the temporary withdrawal of the ego from the physical body. Of course consciousness does not slumber. It must necessarily be functioning somewhere and while the physical body lies inert the consciousness is using the astral body as its vehicle. Sleep is often used as an analogy of death. It is, in very truth, a sort of temporary death, the difference being that the ego is absent from the physical body for a short time instead of permanently.

Every student of occultism is familiar with the fact that when one falls asleep the consciousness leaves the physical body and that the astral body is then its habitation. Hence the living and the so-called dead may then be together. The terror with which some murderers come back into waking consciousness from slumber and their disposition to sometimes automatically go through rehearsals of the murder during sleep are facts that are as commonly known as they are imperfectly understood. In *Macbeth* we are given a most vivid presentation of the fact that sleep thus occultly plunges the murderer back

into the tragedy he foolishly believes to be a
closed chapter—that is, if the murderer happens
to be sensitive enough to bring through into
the waking life the recollection of what has
occurred while he was away from his physical
body when that body was asleep. Neither Macbeth nor Lady Macbeth can sleep soundly and
he speaks of "the affliction of these terrible
dreams that shake us nightly."

Again, the evidence that their sleep is never
peaceful is found in Macbeth's determination to
"make assurance double sure" by removing Banquo from his path,

> That I may tell pale-hearted fear it lies,
> And sleep in spite of thunder.

Just after the murder of the king, he had a
premonition of this coming affliction when, in
Scene II, Act II, he said to Lady Macbeth:

Macbeth:
> Methought I heard a voice cry "Sleep no more!
> Macbeth does murder sleep," the innocent sleep,
> Sleep that knits up the ravell'd sleeve of care,
> The death of each day's life, sore labor's bath,
> Balm of hurt minds, great nature's second course,
> Chief nourisher in life's feast,—

Lady Macbeth:
> What do you mean?

Macbeth:
> Still it cried, "Sleep no more!" to all the house:
> "Glamis hath murder'd sleep, and therefore Caw-
>   dor

Shall sleep no more, Macbeth shall sleep no
    more!"

Bold and resolute as she is, Lady Macbeth
refuses to retire at night without a light burn-
ing. In the sleep-walking scene she rehearses
her part in the murder of the King, trying to
wash the blood from her hands, as she walks.
That is quite comprehensible if we recall her
part in the murder. It will be remembered that
Macbeth was completely unnerved by his crime
and that Lady Macbeth came to his assistance.

Lady Macbeth:
    You do unbend your noble strength to think
    So brainsickly of things. Go get some water,
    And wash this filthy witness from your hand.
    Why did you bring these daggers from the place?
    They must lie there: go carry them, and smear
    The sleepy grooms with blood.
Macbeth:
                                I'll go no more:
    I am afraid to think what I have done;
    Look on't again I dare not.
Lady Macbeth:
                            Infirm of purpose!
    Give me the daggers. The sleeping and the dead
    Are but as pictures; 'tis the eye of childhood
    That fears a painted devil. If he do bleed,
    I'll gild the faces of the grooms withal;
    For it must seem their guilt.
                        [*Exit. Knocking within.*

Macbeth:
    Whence is that knocking?
    How is't with me, when every noise appalls me?
    What hands are here! Ha! they pluck out mine
        eyes.

Will all great Neptune's ocean wash this blood
Clean from my hand? No, this my hand will
   rather
The multitudinous seas incarnadine,
Making the green one red.
           Re-enter Lady Macbeth.

Lady Macbeth:
My hands are of your color, but I shame
To wear a heart so white.—   [*Knocking within.*
               I hear a knocking
At the south entry; retire we to our chamber;
A little water clears us of this deed;
How easy is it, then!

She found, however, that escape from the con-
sequences of crime is not so easy as she imagined.
The murder made an indelible impression on her
brain, and while she sleeps she rises, and her
physical body and brain automatically repeat
fragments of the tragedy.* The gentlewoman
attending Lady Macbeth gives an insight into
what had been occurring nightly. In Scene II,
Act V, we have this:

Doctor:
   How came she by that light?
Gentlewoman:
   Why, it stood by her: she has light by her con-
   tinually; 'tis her command.
Doctor:
   You see, her eyes are open.
Gentlewoman:
   Ay, but their sense is shut.

---

*For a full explanation of the mechanism of conscious-
ness, the classification of dreams, etc., see *Dreams and
Premonitions,* Rogers.

Doctor:
What is it she does now? Look, how she rubs her hands.

Gentlewoman:
It is an accustomed action with her, to seem thus washing her hands. I have known her to continue in this a quarter of an hour.

Lady Macbeth:
Yet here's a spot.

Doctor:
Hark! she speaks. I will set down what comes from her, to satisfy my remembrance the more strongly.

Lady Macbeth:
Out, damned spot! out, I say! One; two: why, then, 'tis time to do't. Hell is murky! Fie, my lord, fie! a soldier, and afeard? What need we fear who knows it, when none can call our power to account? Yet who would have thought the old man to have had so much blood in him?

Doctor:
Do you mark that?

Lady Macbeth:
The Thane of Fife had a wife: where is she now? What! will these hands ne'er be clean? No more o' that, my lord, no more o' that: you mar all with this starting.

Doctor:
Go to, go to; you have known what you should not.

Gentlewoman:
She has spoke what she should not, I am sure of that: Heaven knows what she has known.

Lady Macbeth:
Here's the smell of the blood still: all the perfumes of Arabia will not sweeten this little hand. Oh! Oh! Oh!

Doctor:
What a sigh is there. The heart is sorely charged.

Gentlewoman:
> I would not have such a heart in my bosom for the dignity of the whole body.

Doctor:
> Well, well, well.

Gentlewoman:
> Pray God it be, sir.

Doctor:
> This disease is beyond my practice: yet I have known those which have walked in their sleep who have died holily in their beds.

Lady Macbeth:
> Wash your hands, put on your night-gown; look not so pale. I tell you yet again, Banquo's buried; he cannot come out on's grave.

Doctor:
> Even so?

Lady Macbeth:
> To bed, to bed: there's knocking at the gate. Come, come, come, come, give me your hand. What's done cannot be undone. To bed, to bed, to bed.

The Doctor says truly "This disease is beyond my practice." The wretched woman finally dies under the strain.

Macbeth is a picture, on the material side, of that selfish and heartless ambition in human nature that cruelly sweeps aside remorselessly whatever stands between it and the immediate realization of its desires—the story of ambition, clothed with the power of achievement, and of the terrible reaction that must inevitably follow. It is a presentation of the truth that a structure built upon selfishness and wrong doing is predoomed to be destroyed, regardless the high place and power of its builders, because the seeds of destruction are inherently within it. Every thoughtful reader sees at once that it is remarkably true to life, and the student of things occult sees that it is equally true to the hidden side of nature. The "weird women," the accurate prophecies of coming events, the temporary clairvoyance of Macbeth, the wraith of Banquo, are all as true to nature as are the descriptions and emotions of the various characters which the great dramatist presents. There is nothing in the entire play that is unnatural, untrue or overdrawn. Its various phases of occult phenomena are commonplaces in our own day and may be observed and verified by those who are sufficiently interested to patiently investigate them.

THE TRAGEDY OF KING RICHARD III

The occultism in *Richard III* is to be found chiefly in dreams and these dreams, as presented by the great dramatist, are consistent with the hypothesis that there is an intimate relationship between the physical life and the astral existence.

A brief discussion of the subject of dreams should precede an examination of the terrifying experience of Richard on the eve of the battle that cost him his kingdom and his life. The hypothesis, well known in theosophical literature, is that after the death of the physical body, the consciousness (which is the real man, while the material body is but its temporary vehicle) survives in full integrity in the intangible world which surrounds and permeates the visible world; that that life includes an unbroken memory of this one; that there are several divisions of the invisible world, with varying states of consciousness, from the most dismal purgatory that may properly be called "hell," to an ecstatic state of being that may truly be called "heaven," and that the mental and emotional status of any individual after the loss of the physical body is very definitely determined by the purity or grossness, the benevolence or the malevolence, of his life while in the physical body. Death, however, is not the only method of release from the material realm. Sleep temporarily accomplishes the same result, but it is not often that one retains a memory of what occurs during the brief absence from the physical body, and the infrequent recollections are commonly fragmentary and incoherent. Occasionally, however, the memory is clear and consecutive and, naturally enough, matters of tragic import are strongly impressed on the physical brain by the astral thought and emotion which arise from the deepest joy or the most abject fear.

The terror that comes upon the murderer when in sleep he loses the protection afforded him by the gross physical matter that shuts out the astral world from his waking consciousness, is presented to us in *Richard III*. Of course, not all people are sufficiently sensitive to retain an impression of astral experiences. If it were so every murderer would come back to the waking state more or less unnerved, according to his degree of sensitiveness. Richard seems to have been one of those who occasionally bring into the waking consciousness a very vivid recollection of what had occurred while his consciousness functioned apart from the physical body. He had fallen asleep in his tent, that last night of his life, and had met, as in the flesh, the long list of his victims, each of whom makes it clear that disaster and death are just ahead for him.

The chief distinction between the dream that is a memory, more or less distinct, of an astral experience, and the chaotic dreams that are merely the automatic activity of the brain during slumber, is the vividness and the impression of reality in the former—a characteristic that comes out clearly in the ghost scenes. Richard falls asleep in his tent, Scene III, Act V:

The Ghost of Prince Edward, Son to Henry the Sixth,
rises between the two tents.
Ghost. [*To King Richard*]:
    Let me sit heavy on thy soul to-morrow!
    Think how thou stab'dst me in my prime of youth
    At Tewksbury: despair, therefore, and die!
    Be cheerful, Richmond; for the wronged souls
    Of butcher'd princes fight in thy behalf:
    King Henry's issue, Richmond, comforts thee.
    The Ghost of King Henry the Sixth rises.
Ghost. [*To King Richard*]:
    When I was mortal, my anointed body
    By thee was punched full of deadly holes:
    Think on the Tower and me; despair and die!
    Henry the Sixth bids thee despair and die.

[*To Richmond*]:
  Virtuous and holy, be thou conqueror!
  Harry, that prophesied thou shouldst be the king,
  Doth comfort thee in thy sleep: live thou and
    flourish.
     The Ghost of Clarence rises.

Ghost. [*To King Richard*]:
  Let me sit heavy on thy soul tomorrow!
  I, that was wash'd to death with fulsome wine,
  Poor Clarence, by the guile betray'd to death!
  To-morrow in the battle think on me,
  And fall thy edgeless sword: despair, and die!
[*To Richmond*]:
  Thou offspring of the house of Lancaster,
  The wronged heirs of York do pray for thee:
  Good angels guard thy battle! live, and flourish!
    The Ghosts of Rivers, Grey and Vaughan rise.

Ghost of Rivers. [*To King Richard*]:
  Let me sit heavy on thy soul to-morrow!
  Rivers, that died at Pomfret! despair, and die!

Ghost of Grey. [*To King Richard*]:
  Think upon Grey, and let thy soul despair.

Ghost of Vaughan. [*To King Richard*]:
  Think upon Vaughan, and with guilty fear
  Let fall thy pointless lance: despair, and die!—

All Three. [*To Richmond*]:
  Awake! and think our wrongs in Richard's bosom
  Will conquer him: awake, and win the day!
    The Ghost of Hastings rises.

Ghost. [*To King Richard*]:
  Bloody and guilty, guiltily awake;
  And in a bloody battle end thy days!
  Think on Lord Hastings, so despair, and die!—
[*To Richmond*]:
  Quiet, untroubled soul, awake, awake!
  Arm, fight, and conquer, for fair England's sake!
    The Ghosts of the two young Princes rise.

Ghosts. [*To King Richard*]:
  Dream on thy cousins smother'd in the Tower:
  Let us be lead within thy bosom, Richard,

And weigh thee down to ruin, shame, and death!
Thy nephews' souls bid thee despair, and die!
[*To Richmond*]:
Sleep, Richmond, sleep in peace, and wake in joy;
Good angels guard thee from the boar's annoy!
Live, and beget a happy race of kings!
Edward's unhappy sons do bid thee flourish.
The Ghost of Lady Anne rises.

Ghost. [*To King Richard*]:
Richard, thy wife, that wretched Anne thy wife,
That never slept a quiet hour with thee,
Now fills thy sleep with perturbations:
To-morrow in the battle think on me,
And fall thy edgeless sword: despair, and die!
[*To Richmond*]:
Thou quiet soul, sleep thou a quiet sleep;
Dream of success and happy victory!
Thy adversary's wife doth pray for thee.
The Ghost of Buckingham rises.

Ghost. [*To King Richard*]:
The first was I that help'd thee to the crown;
The last was I that felt thy tyranny.
O! in the battle think on Buckingham,
And die in terror of thy guiltiness!
Dream on, dream on, of bloody deeds and death:
Fainting, despair; despairing, yield thy breath!
[*To Richmond*]:
I died for hope ere I could lend thee aid:
But cheer thy heart, and be thou not dismay'd:
God and good angels fight on Richmond's side;
And Richard falls in height of all his pride.
*The Ghosts vanish. King Richard starts out of his
dream.*

King Richard:
Give me another horse! bind up my wounds!
Have mercy, Jesu! Soft! I did but dream.

So real is all this to Richard that when he
awakens he is not, at first, able to distinguish
the astral from the physical. A dream which is

merely the result of the automatic activity of the physical brain and its etheric counterpart is likely to be chaotic and not very life-like; but a dream that is a memory of a real astral experience has vividness as one of its chief characteristics although it may be fragmentary. It has the essence of reality, and it is as real as events in physical life. The late Richard Mansfield used to bring this out admirably when playing the role of the murderous king. "Who's there?" he demands, as Ratcliff approaches, and the reply is "Ratcliff, my lord; 'tis I"; but Richard doubts his senses. Slowly and fearfully he approaches Ratcliff, stretching out his arm to the utmost, advancing by inches, and making sure by the sense of touch that this is really a being of flesh. Finally assured of this, he falls limply upon his lieutenant's shoulder and exclaims:

> O Ratcliff! I have dream'd a fearful dream.
> What thinkest thou, will our friends prove all
>   true?

Ratcliff:
> No doubt, my lord.

King Richard:
> O Ratcliff! I fear, I fear,—

Ratcliff:
> Nay, good my lord, be not afraid of shadows.

King Richard:
> By the apostle Paul, shadows to-night
> Have struck more terror to the soul of Richard

Than can the substance of ten thousand soldiers
Armed in proof, and led by shallow Richmond.

In his soliloquy before Ratcliff appeared he
had said:

Methought the souls of all that I had murder'd
Came to my tent and everyone did threat
To-morrow's vengeance on the head of Richard.

These ghosts in *Richard III* are none the less
ghosts because they are met in dreamland—that
is, they are as much the individuals represented
as in the case of the ghost of Hamlet's father. In
each case they are *people*, living now in bodies
of astral matter instead of physical matter, and
they are precisely the same sort of people they
were before they lost their physical bodies—
neither better nor worse. They are all actuated
by the same motives and emotions that move
living people. Indeed, they *are* living people,
but are no longer living in physical bodies. If
all of these eleven who terrorize Richard had
been back in the material world again, they
would have spoken and acted in precisely the
manner they are represented to have done. They
have not suddenly become forgiving angels because they have passed out of the material
world, but are quite as human as when they
walked the streets of London.

In strong contrast with the dream of Richard is that of Richmond. When his lieutenants call upon him in the morning and ask

> How have you slept my lord?

He replies:

> The sweetest sleep, the fairest-boding dreams
> That ever enter'd in a drowsy head,
> Have I since your departure had, my lords.
> Methought their souls, whose bodies Richard
>   murder'd,
> Came to my tent and cried on victory:
> I promise you, my heart is very jocund
> In the remembrance of so fair a dream.

The latter part of Richard's dream has a close relationship to impending events. As he is awakening, he exclaims:

> Give me another horse! bind up my wounds!

In Scene IV of the last Act we have this:

Catesby:
> Rescue, my lord of Norfolk! rescue, rescue!
> The king enacts more wonders than a man,
> Daring an opposite to every danger:
> His horse is slain, and all on foot he fights,
> Seeking for Richmond in the throat of death.
> Rescue, fair lord, or else the day is lost!
>   *Alarum.   Enter King Richard.*

King Richard:
> A horse! a horse! my kingdom for a horse!

Catesby:
> Withdraw, my lord; I'll help you to a horse.

King Richard:
> Slave! I have set my life upon a cast,
> And I will stand the hazard of the die.
> I think there be six Richmonds in the field;

> Five have I slain to-day, instead of him,—
> A horse! a horse! my kingdom for a horse!

It is a favorite theory of materialistic psychologists that, although a dream may apparently forecast future events, a close examination will show that there was something in the mind of the dreamer which will account for the apparent knowledge of the future. No such explanation is possible in the dream of the Duke of Clarence, while confined in London Tower, for it *is true to facts of which he is entirely ignorant.* His brother, Richard, not yet king, was plotting the death of Clarence and soon brought it about; but with such devilish cunning did he manage the matter that his victim had not the slightest suspicion of the fact. In the dream, however, as in reality, Richard is the indirect, but actual cause of his brother's death. Richard, then Duke of Gloucester, scheming to ascend the throne, muses as follows at the beginning of the play:

> Plots have I laid, inductions dangerous,
> By drunken prophecies, libels, and dreams,
> To set my brother Clarence and the king
> In deadly hate the one against the other;
> And if King Edward be as true and just
> As I am subtle, false, and treacherous,
> This day should Clarence closely be mew'd up,
> About a prophecy, which says, that G
> Of Edward's heirs the murderer shall be.

Clarence has the greatest confidence in Richard. He does not know that his commitment to the Tower is the result of Richard's lies to King Edward, but thinks it is wholly the work of the king. When Clarence is pleading for his life with his murderers, sent by Richard, in Scene IV of Act I, the following conversation takes place:

First Murderer:
    Who made thee then a bloody minister,
    When gallant-springing, brave Plantagenet,
    That princely novice, was struck dead by thee?

Clarence:
    My brother's love, the devil, and my rage.

First Murderer:
    Thy brother's love, our duty, and thy fault,
    Provoke us hither now to slaughter thee.

Clarence:
    If you do love my brother, hate not me;
    I am his brother, and I love him well.
    If you are hir'd for meed, go back again,
    And I will send you to my brother Gloucester,
    Who shall reward you better for my life
    Than Edward will for tidings of my death.

Second Murderer:
    You are deceiv'd, your brother Gloucester hates
      you.

Clarence:
    Oh, no! he loves me, and he holds me dear:
    Go you to him from me.

Both Murderers:
    Ay, so we will.

Clarence:
    Tell him, when our princely father York
    Bless'd his three sons with his victorious arm,
    And charg'd us from his soul to love each other,
    He little thought of this divided friendship:
    Bid Gloucester think on this, and he will weep.

First Murderer:
    Ay, millstones; as he lesson'd us to weep.
Clarence:
    O! do not slander him, for he is kind.
First Murderer:
    Right;
    As snow in harvest. Thou deceiv'st thyself:
    'Tis he that sends us to destroy you here.
Clarence:
    It cannot be: for he bewept my fortune,
    And hugg'd me in his arms, and swore, with sobs,
    That he would labour my delivery.

The dream which preceded the murder is fully narrated in Scene IV, Act I. It will be noted that the two essential points in it are the distress of drowning and the association of Richard with the cause of death.

Brackenbury:
    Why looks your Grace so heavily to-day?
Clarence:
    O, I have pass'd a miserable night,
    So full of ugly sights, of ghastly dreams,
    That, as I am a Christian faithful man,
    I would not spend another such a night,
    Though 'twere to buy a world of happy days,
    So full of dismal terror was the time.
Brakenbury:
    What was your dream, my lord? I pray you,
        tell me.
Clarence:
    Methought that I had broken from the Tower,
    And was embark'd to cross to Burgundy;
    And in my company, my brother Gloucester,
    Who from my cabin tempted me to walk
    Upon the hatches: thence we look'd toward Eng-
        land,
    And cited up a thousand heavy times,

During the wars of York and Lancaster,
That had befall'n us. As we pac'd along
Upon the giddy footing of the hatches,
Methought that Gloucester stumbled; and, in
    falling,
Struck me, that thought to stay him, overboard,
Into the tumbling billows of the main.
Lord, Lord! methought what pain it was to
    drown:
What dreadful noise of water in mine ears!
What sights of ugly death within mine eyes!
Methought I saw a thousand fearful wracks;
A thousand men that fishes gnaw'd upon;
Wedges of gold, great anchors, heaps of pearl,
Inestimable stones, unvalu'd jewels,
All scatter'd in the bottom of the sea.
Some lay in dead men's skulls; and in those holes,
Where eyes did once inhabit, there were crept,
As 'twere in scorn of eyes, reflecting gems,
That woo'd the slimy bottom of the deep,
And mocked the dead bones that lay scatter'd by.

Brakenbury:
Had you such leisure in the time of death
To gaze upon those secrets of the deep?

Clarence:
Methought I had; and often did I strive
To yield the ghost; but still the envious flood
Stopt in my soul, and would not let it forth
To find the empty, vast, and wandering air;
But smother'd it within my panting bulk,
Which almost burst to belch it in the sea.

This conversation with Brakenbury was immediately preceding the entrance of the assassins who killed Clarence.

The latter part of the dream, as disclosed in the conversation with Brakenbury, dealt with life after bodily death, an experience, which, at

the time of the dream, he was soon to pass
through, and the student of after death conditions will attest the accuracy of the descriptions.
The dream outlined the fate that naturally
awaits one who had followed the course con-
fessed to by the duke.

Brakenbury:
    Awak'd you not with this sore agony?
Clarence:
    No, no, my dream was lengthen'd after life;
    O! then began the tempest to my soul.
    I pass'd, methought, the melancholy flood,
    With that grim ferryman which poets write of,
    Unto the kingdom of perpetual night.
    The first that there did greet my stranger soul,
    Was my great father-in-law, renowned Warwick;
    Who cried aloud, "What scourge for perjury
    Can this dark monarchy afford false Clarence?"
    And so he vanish'd: then came wandering by
    A shadow like an angel, with bright hair
    Dabbled in blood; and he shriek'd out aloud,
    "Clarence is come,—false, fleeting, perjur'd Clar-
        ence,
    That stabbed me in the field by Tewksbury;—
    Seize on him! Furies, take him unto torment."
    With that, methought, a legion of foul fiends
    Environ'd me, and howled in mine ears
    Such hideous cries, that, with the very noise
    I trembling wak'd, and, for a season after
    Could not believe but that I was in hell,
    Such terrible impression made my dream.
Brakenbury:
    No marvel, lord, though it affrighted you;
    I am afraid, methinks, to hear you tell it.
Clarence:
    O Brakenbury! I have done these things
    That now give evidence against my soul,

> For Edward's sake; and see how he requites me.
> O God! if my deep prayers cannot appease thee,
> But thou wilt be aveng'd on my misdeeds,
> Yet execute thy wrath on me alone:
> O! spare my guiltless wife and my poor children.

Near the close of the first act, we have this:

Second Murderer:
> Look behind you, my lord.

First Murderer: [*Stabs him*]
> Take that, and that: if all this will not do,
> I'll drown you in the malmsey-butt within.

Evidently when he carries away the body, the duke is not dead, for the usual stage direction "dies" does not follow. In the ghost scene in the last act, as already narrated, the ghost of Clarence says:

> I, that was wash'd to death with fulsome wine.

In the dream of Clarence, we have an instance in which there was no fact known to the waking consciousness to account for the dream which forecast approaching death. With absolute confidence in the love and loyalty of his brother, Richard, Clarence nevertheless brought back from the dream state of consciousness the fact that Richard was the cause of Clarence's death —that he "tempted" him "to walk upon the hatches" and then stumbled against him and hurled him overboard to his death.

Lord Stanley had a dream that served as a warning, the ignoring of which cost Lord Hastings his life. How deeply that dream had impressed Stanley may be inferred from the fact that his messenger arrived at Hastings' house at four o'clock in the morning.

In Scene II, Act III, we have the following:

Messenger: [*Knocking*]
    My lord! my lord!
Hastings: [*Within*]
    Who knocks?
Messenger:
    One from the Lord Stanley.
Hastings: [*Within*]
    What is't o'clock?
Messenger:
    Upon the stroke of four.
                  Enter Hastings.
Hastings:
    Cannot my Lord Stanley sleep these tedious
        nights?
Messenger:
    So it appears by that I have to say.
    First, he commends me to your noble self.
Hastings:
    What then?
Messenger:
    Then certifies your lordship, that this night
    He dreamt the boar had razed off his helm:
    Besides, he says there are two councils held;
    And that may be determin'd at the one
    Which may make you and him to rue at the
        other.
    Therefore he sends to know your lordship's pleas-
        ure,
    If you will presently take horse with him,

> And with all speed post with him towards the
>   north,
> To shun the danger that his soul divines.

Hastings treated the matter lightly—a course which he was soon to bitterly regret. No sense of danger troubles him and he says to Stanley's messenger:

> Go, fellow, go, return unto thy lord;
> Bid him not fear the separated councils:
> His honour and myself are at the one,
> And at the other is my good friend Catesby;
> Where nothing can proceed that toucheth us
> Whereof I shall not have intelligence.
> Tell him his fears are shallow, wanting instance:
> And for his dreams, I wonder he's so fond
> To trust the mockery of unquiet slumbers.
> To fly the boar before the boar pursues,
> Were to incense the boar to follow us
> And make pursuit where he did mean no chase.
> Go, bid thy master rise and come to me;
> And we will both together to the Tower,
> Where, he shall see, the boar will use us kindly.

When Stanley himself arrived later, Hastings greeted him jocularly with

> Come on, come on; where is your boar-spear,
>   man?
> Fear you the boar, and go so unprovided?

Stanley, however, had been so deeply moved by the dream that he is much depressed and protests that while Hastings "may jest on," the situation is sufficiently serious. They went together to the consultation in the Tower with

Richard and others, about the coronation of the little prince. There, Richard suddenly turned on Hastings, and with no ground whatever for his course, except that Hastings was loyal to the rightful heir, ordered Lord Hastings' immediate execution. Stanley avoided a similar fate only by pretending to acquiesce in Richard's plans. Had his real position been known, he would have been sent to the block with Hastings. How narrowly he finally escaped and how true to the facts was the dream that the boar "razed off his helm," comes vividly out in Scene IV of Act IV. Richard, then king, has a conversation with Stanley:

King Richard:
    My mind is chang'd. Stanley, what news with
        you?
Stanley:
    None good, my liege, to please you with the
        hearing;
    Nor none so bad but well may be reported.
King Richard:
    Heyday, a riddle! neither good nor bad!
    What need'st thou run so many miles about,
    When thou mayst tell thy tale the nearest way?
    Once more, what news?
Stanley:
    Richmond is on the seas.
King Richard:
    There let him sink, and be the seas on him!
    White-liver'd runagate! what doth he there?
Stanley:
    I know not, mighty sovereign, but by guess.

King Richard:
 Well, as you guess?

Stanley:
 Stirr'd up by Dorset, Buckingham, and Morton,
 He makes for England, here to claim the crown.

King Richard:
 Is the chair empty? Is the sword unsway'd?
 Is the king dead? the empire unpossessed?
 What heir of York is there alive but we?
 And who is England's king but great York's
  heir?
 Then, tell me, what makes he upon the seas?

Stanley:
 Unless for that, my liege, I cannot guess.

King Richard:
 Unless for that he comes to be your liege,
 You cannot guess wherefore the Welshman comes.
 Thou wilt revolt and fly to him I fear.

Stanley:
 No, my good lord; therefore mistrust me not.
King Richard:
 Where is thy power then to beat him back?
 Where be thy tenants and thy followers?
 Are they not now upon the western shore,
 Safe-conducting the rebels from their ships?

Stanley:
 No, my good lord, my friends are in the north.
King Richard:
 Cold friends to me: what do they in the north
 When they should serve their sovereign in the
  west?

Stanley:
 They have not been commanded, mighty king:
 Pleaseth your majesty to give me leave,
 I'll muster up my friends, and meet your Grace,
 Where and what time your majesty shall please.
King Richard:
 Ay, ay, thou wouldst be gone to join with Rich-
  mond:
 But I'll not trust thee.

Stanley:
> Most mighty sovereign,
> You have no cause to hold my friendship doubt-
>   ful.
> I never was nor never will be false.

King Richard:
> Go then and muster men: but leave behind
> Your son, George Stanley: look your heart be
>   firm,
> Or else his head's assurance is but frail.

Evidently Richard shrewdly guessed Stanley's inner thought and real intention, and only the hope that he could be compelled to support Richard through fear for young Stanley's life prevented Richard dealing as summarily with Lord Stanley as he had with Hastings. It was a very narrow missing of death by the fangs of "the boar."

In the last scene of that act, Stanley says:

> Sir Christopher, tell Richmond this from me:
> That in the sty of this most bloody boar
> My son George Stanley is frank'd up in hold:
> If I revolt, off goes young George's head;
> The fear of that holds off my present aid.

As Richard's last battle is about to begin, he says to the returned messenger:

> What says Lord Stanley? will he bring his power?

Messenger:
> My lord, he doth deny to come.

King Richard:
> Off with his son George's head!

Norfolk:
> My lord, the enemy is pass'd the marsh:
> After the battle let George Stanley die.

Even thus narrowly does the son also escape, for Richard is himself slain and young Stanley is released. The circumstances very accurately fit the dream in which the "boar" brought the dreamer so close to death that his helmet was knocked off by the beast.

It will be seen that the dream of Lord Stanley also accurately revealed other things. Richard, then Duke of Gloucester, Buckingham and Catesby, had held a conference on the subject of the possibility of winning Hastings and Stanley to their course, and Richard had taken the ground that if Hastings could not be won over he should be summarily killed as he soon afterward was. In Scene I of Act III, Buckingham says to Catesby:

> What think'st thou? is it not an easy matter
> To make William Lord Hastings of our mind,
> For the instalment of this noble duke
> In the seat royal of this famous isle?

Catesby:
> He for his father's sake so loves the prince
> That he will not be won to aught against him.

Buckingham:
> What think'st thou then of Stanley? what will he?

Catesby:
> He will do all in all as Hastings doth.

Buckingham:
> Well then, no more but this: go, gentle Catesby,
> And, as it were far off, sound thou Lord Hastings,
> How he doth stand affected to our purpose;

And summon him to-morrow to the Tower,
To sit about the coronation.
If thou dost find him tractable to us,
Encourage him, and tell him all our reasons:
If he be leaden, icy-cold, unwilling,
Be thou so too, and so break off the talk,
And give us notice of his inclination;
For we to-morrow hold divided councils,
Wherein thyself shalt highly be employ'd.

Gloucester:

Commend me to Lord William: tell him, Catesby,
His ancient knot of dangerous adversaries
To-morrow are let blood at Pomfret Castle;
And bid my lord, for joy of this good news,
Give Mistress Shore one gentle kiss the more.

Buckingham:

Good Catesby, go, effect this business soundly.

Catesby:

My good lords both, with all the heed I can.

Gloucester:

Shall we hear from you, Catesby, ere we sleep?

Catesby:

You shall, my lord.

Gloucester:

At Crosby-place, there shall you find us both.

                            [Exit Catesby.

Buckingham:

Now, my lord, what shall we do if we perceive
Lord Hastings will not yield to our complots?

Gloucester:

Chop off his head.

The accuracy with which Stanley's dream forecast impending events is found in the lines

Besides, he says there are two councils held;
And that may be determined at the one
Which may make you and me to rue at the
other.

At the conference between the duke, Bucking-

ham and Catesby, the decision was reached that
cost Hastings his life at the second council on the
subject of the coronation—a fate which Hastings would apparently have escaped if he had
accepted Stanley's proposition to "take horse
with him" in order "to shun the danger that his
soul divines." Instead, he scoffed at the warning with the fatal words to the messenger,

> Go, fellow, go, return unto thy lord;
> Bid him not fear the separated councils.

The great dramatist has here presented the
story of a dream that warned against an impending danger—a symbolical dream in which
the boar is Richard. The language used shows
that both men understood the symbol perfectly.
Hastings challenges his friend to go with him
to the Tower "where he shall see, the boar will
treat us kindly." It is interesting to note that
Stanley's dream disclosed nothing about the fate
of Hastings but only that he himself was
brought very near to death by the boar. Stanley's dream apparently furnished a warning of
imminent danger that, had it been heeded, would
have saved Hasting's life.

JULIUS CAESAR

The occult phenomena in *Julius Caesar* include a ghost, a soothsayer, and a remarkable symbolical dream. The forecasting of the impending tragedy begins in Scene II of Act I. Caesar, with a procession of attendants and followers, is on the way to the race-course, and in the crowd is a soothsayer, who later speaks of himself as "a feeble man." As the procession moves forward with music, there comes the interruption from the soothsayer:

Soothsayer:
    Caesar!
Caesar:
    Ha! Who calls?
Casca:
    Bid every noise be still: peace yet again!
                  [*Music ceases.*
Caesar:
    Who is it in the press who calls on me?
    I hear a tongue, shriller than all the music,
    Cry "Caesar." Speak; Caesar is turn'd to hear.
Soothsayer:
    Beware the ides of March.
Caesar:
                  What man is that?
Brutus:
    A soothsayer bids you beware the ides of March.

Caesar:
Set him before me; let me see his face.
Casca:
Fellow, come from the throng; look upon Caesar.
Caesar:
What sayst thou to me now? Speak once again.
Soothsayer:
Beware the ides of March.
Caesar:
He is a dreamer; let us leave him: pass.

It is evident, from the remark of Brutus, that the man who gave this friendly warning was known to him as a soothsayer but, although Caesar was accustomed to consulting those supposed to be skilled in occult lore, as Scene II in Act II discloses, he paid no attention to the solemn and repeated warning of the soothsayer. He dismisses the incident with the remark that the soothsayer is "a dreamer." It is interesting to note here that the warning given by the soothsayer correctly names the date on which the assassination later takes place. It might be argued that he may have had some actual knowledge of the conspirators' plans, but such an explanation is precluded by Portia's conversation with him in Scene IV of Act II.

Portia:
Come, hither, fellow: which way hast thou been?
Soothsayer:
At mine own house, good lady.

Portia:
> What is 't o'clock?

Soothsayer:
> About the ninth hour, lady.

Portia:
> Is Caesar yet gone to the Capitol?

Soothsayer:
> Madam, not yet: I go to take my stand,
> To see him pass on to the Capitol.

Portia:
> Thou hast some suit to Caesar, hast thou not?

Soothsayer:
> That I have, lady: if it will please Caesar
> To be so good to Caesar as to hear me,
> I shall beseech him to befriend himself.

Portia:
> Why, know'st thou any harm's intended towards
> him?

Soothsayer:
> None that I know will be, much that I fear may
> chance.

It is immediately after this conversation, in the beginning of Act III, that Caesar appears in the street before the Capitol, with a crowd following. The soothsayer has posted himself in a conspicuous place and Caesar, seeing and recognizing him as the prophet who had given him warning, calls out, apparently in derision of that warning,

> The ides of March are come.

With a dramatic significance, the soothsayer replies:

> Ay, Caesar; but not gone.

In other words, there was still time for something to happen on the ides of March. That was the soothsayer's final warning; within an hour, Caesar was dead.

From a different source, and in a wholly different way, the future of Caesar is foreshadowed. His wife, Calphurnia, had a very remarkable symbolical dream during the night preceding the assassination. It will be remembered that the conspirators wished to feel sure that Caesar would appear at the Capitol. Cassius expressed apprehension on that point:

Cassius: But it is doubtful yet
Whether Caesar will come forth to-day or no;
For he is superstitious grown of late,
Quite from the main opinion he held once
Of fantasy, of dreams, and ceremonies.
It may be these apparent prodigies,
The unaccustom'd terror of this night,
And the persuasion of his augurers,
May hold him from the Capitol to-day,

Decius proposes a plan:

Decius:
Never fear that: if he be so resolv'd
I can o'ersway him; for he loves to hear
That unicorns may be betray'd with trees,
And bears with glasses, elephants with holes,
Lions with toils, and men with flatterers;
But when I tell him he hates flatterers,
He says he does, being then most flattered.
Let me work;

> For I can give his humour the true bent,
> And I will bring him to the Capitol.
> *Cassius*:
> Nay, we will all of us be there to fetch him.

In pursuance of this arrangement, Decius went ahead of the others, and truly enough, discovered that Caesar had decided that he would not go to the Capitol. This came about because of Calphurnia's dream. It had made a great impression upon her. She says:

> What mean you, Caesar? Think you to walk forth?
> You shall not stir out of your house to-day.

But he was not easily persuaded, and replies:

> Caesar shall forth: the things that threaten'd me
> Ne'er look'd but on my back; when they shall see
> The face of Caesar, they are vanished.

Calphurnia continues to plead, and their conversation is interrupted by the entrance of the servant who had been sent to the priests for their opinions.

Caesar:
> What say the augurers?
Servant:
> They would not have you to stir forth to-day.
> Plucking the entrails of an offering forth,
> They could not find a heart within the beast.
Caesar:
> The gods do this in shame of cowardice:

Caesar should be a beast without a heart
If he should stay at home to-day for fear.
No, Caesar shall not; danger knows full well
That Caesar is more dangerous than he:
We are two lions litter'd in one day,
And I the elder and more terrible:
And Caesar shall go forth.

Calphurnia:
Alas! my lord,
Your wisdom is consum'd in confidence.
Do not go forth to-day: call it my fear
That keeps you in the house, and not your own.
We'll send Mark Antony to the senate-house,
And he shall say you are not well to-day:
Let me, upon my knee, prevail in this.

Caesar:
Mark Antony shall say I am not well;
And, for thy humour, I will stay at home.
Here's Decius Brutus, he shall tell them so.

Decius:
Caesar, all hail! Good morrow, worthy Caesar:
I come to fetch you to the senate-house.

Caesar:
And you are come in very happy time
To bear my greeting to the senators,
And tell them that I will not come to-day:
Cannot, is false, and that I dare not, falser;
I will not come today: tell them so, Decius.

Calphurnia:
Say he is sick.

Caesar:
Shall Caesar send a lie?
Have I in conquest stretch'd mine arm so far
To be afeard to tell greybeards the truth?
Decius, go tell them Caesar will not come.

Decius:
Most mighty Caesar, let me know some cause,
Lest I be laugh'd at when I tell them so.

Caesar:
The cause is in my will: I will not come;
That is enough to satisfy the senate:

> But for your private satisfaction,
> Because I love you, I will let you know:
> Calphurnia here, my wife, stays me at home:
> She dreamt to-night she saw my statua,
> Which, like a fountain with a hundred spouts,
> Did run pure blood; and many lusty Romans
> Came smiling, and did bathe their hands in it:
> And these does she apply for warnings and por-
>   tents,
> And evils imminent; and on her knee
> Hath begg'd that I will stay at home to-day.

So cleverly did Decius appeal to Caesar's pride and vanity that he soon changed his mind. How, reasoned Decius, could he satisfactorily explain to the senate Caesar's refusal to come. How would it sound to say that the great Caesar was governed by a woman's dream! And thus, before the other conspirators had arrived, Caesar, listening to the plausible sophistry of Decius, exclaims:

> How foolish do your fears seem now, Calphurnia!
> I am ashamed I did yield to them.
> Give me my robe, for I will go.

What happened at the Capitol fulfilled to the letter Calphurnia's symbolical dream. When Caesar fell, with blood gushing from a score of wounds, the senate and the crowd of citizens that had gathered were, naturally enough, thrown into a state of panic. To one of the senators, Cassius says:

> And leave us, Publius; lest that the people,
> Rushing on us, should do your age some mischief.

The assassins saw that it was necessary to devise some way of presenting their case to the populace—some method of indicating that they had acted from patriotic motives. It was Brutus who thought of a plan. As they stood about the body of Caesar, Brutus said:

> Stoop, Romans, stoop,
> And let us bathe our hands in Caesar's blood
> Up to the elbows, and besmear our swords:
> Then walk we forth, even to the market-place;
> And waving our red weapons o'er our heads,
> Let's all cry, "Peace, freedom, and liberty!"

Calphurnia had dreamed that Caesar's statue had changed to a fountain which ran "pure blood," instead of water; that it had numerous spouts;* that "many lusty Romans came smiling and did bathe their hands in it." The dream presented, symbolically, exactly what occurred, even to the emotion of satisfaction felt by the conspirators in Caesar's death. Moreover, the dream is directly connected by the dramatist with the tragedy which it prophesies.

In Scene II of Act II, in his house Caesar ap-

---

* Octavius refers to "Caesar's three and thirty wounds."
(Scene I, Act V.)

pears in night-dress, having just arisen, and
soliloquizes:

> Nor heaven nor earth have been at peace to-
>   night:
> Thrice hath Calphurnia in her sleep cried out,
> "Help, ho! They murder Caesar!"

It could not be made plainer that in the dream
state of consciousness, Calphurnia got the full
import of the approaching assassination of her
husband.

Nothing can be clearer than the intention of
the great dramatist to show that future events
sometimes "cast their shadows before" in various
ways—that they may make their impress upon
the human consciousness. In the case of the
soothsayer, it is a sense of impending danger, but
it is devoid of detail, except as to date, which is
very definite. In the symbolical dream, however, it is extremely definite, with details exactly
corresponding to the facts as they later trans-
pired. Shakespeare treats the whole matter
seriously, and it is impossible to believe that an
author would, in the working out of the play,
verify such occult phenomena to the very letter,
unless he believed that he was thus presenting
truths of nature.

The ghosts of the Shakespeare plays are

rational and natural ghosts. There is always a reason for their appearance, just as there is a reason back of every act of a sane person. The dead king who materializes in *Hamlet* naturally had an intense desire to acquaint his son with the truth about the murder and the fact of his uncle's diabolical treachery. In *Richard III* the murder victims, thrust suddenly from their physical bodies by the ever ready blade of the conscienceless Gloucester, naturally enough hated him as they would had they remained alive in prison in physical life, while he swaggered about with the crown. It is not strange that they should be pleased with his coming downfall and the warning they gave him, which is a warning to dishearten instead of to save, is most natural. It contains a note of triumph. They see his death and do all they can to make it doubly sure.

Between Caesar and Brutus there had been so strong a tie that when Caesar discovers Brutus among his assassins he exclaims in astonishment, "Thou too, Brutus?—then fall, Caesar!" Whether when he materialized in Brutus' tent it was in the role of friend to warn him of approaching death, and thus lessen the shock by reflection upon the inevitable, or in the role of enemy, it is, in either case, a perfectly natural thing. If his love for Brutus had suddenly changed to enmity when he saw him as one of his slayers, and he was unforgiving, Brutus would be the object of Caesar's resentment, and in that case it might easily be that he came as avenger. But if he felt more sorrow than anger and his affection for this "noblest Roman of them all," as even his enemies called Brutus, remained strong despite his error of joining the conspirators, then it is most natural that Caesar should be drawn to him with a friendly word on what was coming.

The ghost in *Julius Caesar* is less interesting than the ghosts in *Hamlet, Macbeth* and *Richard III*. It plays a minor part, and here there can be no plea by materialists that it is introduced either as a necessary dramatic factor, or as a medium for the externalization of the thoughts of anybody. The ghost appears in Scene III of Act IV:

Brutus:
> Let me see, let me see; is not the leaf turn'd down
> Where I left reading? Here it is, I think.
> *Enter the Ghost of Caesar.*
> How ill this taper burns! Ha! who comes here?
> I think it is the weakness of mine eyes
> That shapes this monstrous apparition.
> It comes upon me. Art thou any thing?

Art thou some god, some angel, or some devil,
That mak'st my blood cold and my hair to stare?
Speak to me what thou art.

Ghost:
Thy evil spirit, Brutus.

Brutus:
                              Why com'st thou?

Ghost:
To tell thee thou shalt see me at Philippi.

Brutus:
Well; then I shall see thee again?

Ghost:
Ay, at Philippi.

Brutus:
Why, I will see thee at Philippi then.
                              [*Ghost vanishes.*

Attention has previously been called to the fact that it is when one is overwrought, when nerve tension is high, that the possibility of super-physical sight is greatest. Brutus had just had a violent quarrel with Cassius, followed by the reaction of pledging renewed friendship, when the ghost appeared. The ghost says little—that Brutus shall see him at Philippi, and so he did. When, with a few friends (in his own words, "poor remains of friends") Brutus sat on a rock and solicited death at their hands, he has the following conversation with Volumnius:

Brutus:
Come hither, good Volumnius: list a word.

Volumnius:
What says my lord?

Brutus:
> Why this, Volumnius:
> The ghost of Caesar hath appear'd to me
> Two several times by night; at Sardis once,
> And this last night here in Philippi fields.
> I know my hour is come.

Brutus apparently regarded Caesar's ghost as an avenger. Cassius came to a tragic end through a misunderstanding. Victory was mistaken for defeat by Pindarus who reported to Cassius that Titinius was taken. The erroneous report led to Cassius' death, by his own sword, at his own command, in the hands of his servant, and Cassius exclaims:

> Caesar, thou art reveng'd,
> Even with the sword that kill'd thee.

When Titinius sees the body, and realizes the cause of the tragedy he takes up Cassius' sword and kills himself. When the bodies of the two, Cassius and Titinius, are discovered by Brutus and his party, Brutus, looking down upon the suicides, exclaims:

> O Julius Caesar! thou art mighty yet!
> Thy spirit walks abroad, and turns our swords
> In our own proper entrails.

When in Scene V of Act V, Brutus runs upon his sword, held in the hands of Strato by Brutus' command, he exclaims:

> Caesar, now be still;
> I kill'd not thee with half so good a will.

What the ghost of Caesar had to say on its final appearance to Brutus at Philippi, the reader is left by the dramatist to imagine, but there is no room for doubt about the impression it made upon Brutus. He was utterly weary of life,—a hunted and a haunted man.

TROILUS AND CRESSIDA

The tragic fate of Hector in *Troilus and Cressida* furnishes one of the best examples of prophecy in any of the Shakespeare plays. His sister foretells it, his wife dreams of it and his mother has visions of it.

In Scene II, Act II, the Trojan King and his sons Hector, Troilus, Paris and Helenus are debating the question of returning Helen in compliance with the Greek demand or of continuing the war when the King's daughter Cassandra enters:

Cassandra [*Within*]:

                  Cry, Trojans, cry!

Priam: What noise? what shriek?

Troilus:

    'Tis our mad sister, I do know her voice.

Cassandra [*Within*]:

                  Cry, Trojans!

Hector:

    It is Cassandra.

          Enter Cassandra, raving.

Cassandra:

    Cry, Trojans, cry! lend me ten thousand eyes,
    And I will fill them with prophetic tears.

Hector:

    Peace, sister, peace!

Cassandra:

    Virgins and boys, mid-age and wrinkled,

> Soft infancy, that nothing canst but cry,
> Add to my clamours! let us pay betimes
> A moiety of that mass of moan to come.
> Cry, Trojans, cry! practise your eyes with tears!
> Troy must not be, nor goodly Ilion stand;
> Our firebrand brother, Paris, burns us all.
> Cry, Trojans, cry! a Helen and a woe!
> Cry, cry! Troy burns or else let Helen go.

Hector has been arguing that Helen should be returned, and after Cassandra's pronouncement he turns to Troilus and says:

Hector:
> Now, youthful Troilus, do not these high strains
> Of divination in our sister work
> Some touches of remorse? or is your blood
> So madly hot that no discourse of reason,
> Nor fear of bad success in a bad cause,
> Can qualify the same?

The argument continues and the war party finally wins the day. On the morning of the fatal day when Prince Hector last went forth to fight the Greeks, Andromache, his wife, Cassandra, his sister, and Priam, his father, all pleaded in vain against his decision. Andromache, like Caesar's wife, had dreamed of impending tragedy, though not in detail as Calphurnia had done. In Scene III, Act V, we have this:

> *Enter Hector and Andromache.*

Andromache:
> When was my lord so much ungently temper'd,
> To stop his ears against admonishment?
> Unarm, unarm, and do not fight to-day.

Hector:
> You train me to offend you; get you in:
> By all the everlasting gods, I'll go.

Andromache:
> My dreams will, sure, prove ominous to the day.

Hector:
> No more, I say.

> > *Enter Cassandra.*

Cassandra:
> Where is my brother Hector?

Andromache:
> Here, sister; arm'd, and bloody in intent.
> Consort with me in loud and dear petition;
> Pursue we him on knees; for I have dream'd
> Of bloody turbulence, and this whole night
> Hath nothing been but shapes and forms of
> > slaughter.

Cassandra:
> O! 'tis true.

Hector:
> > Ho! bid my trumpet sound.

Cassandra:
> No notes of sally, for the heavens, sweet brother.

Hector:
> Be gone, I say: the gods have heard me swear.

Cassandra:
> The gods are deaf to hot and peevish vows:
> They are polluted offerings, more abhorr'd
> Than spotted livers in the sacrifice.

Andromache:
> O! be persuaded: do not count it holy
> To hurt by being just: it is as lawful,
> For we would give much, to use violent thefts,
> And rob in the behalf of charity.

Cassandra:
> It is the purpose that makes strong the vow;
> But vows to every purpose must not hold.
> Unarm, sweet Hector.

Hector:
> > Hold you still, I say;
> Mine honour keeps the weather of my fate:
> Life every man holds dear; but the dear man

Holds honour far more precious-dear than life.
> *Enter Troilus.*
How now, young man! mean'st thou to fight
to-day?

Andromache:
Cassandra, call my father to persuade.
> [*Exit Cassandra.*]

Cassandra had been referred to by Troilus as "our mad sister." Prophets are quite often thought to be mad and some of them may be; but Cassandra talks with perfect sanity and good sense. She is tremendously moved by the approaching fate of her brother which she regards as a certainty if he goes out to fight, but there is no insanity in her words:

> *Re-enter Cassandra, with Priam.*

Cassandra:
Lay hold upon him, Priam, hold him fast:
He is thy crutch; now if thou lose thy stay,
Thou on him leaning, and all Troy on thee,
Fall all together.

Priam:
Come, Hector, come; go back:
Thy wife hath dream'd; thy mother hath had
visions;
Cassandra doth foresee; and I myself
Am like a prophet suddenly enrapt,
To tell thee that this day is ominous:
Therefore, come back.

Hector:
Aeneas is a-field;
And I do stand engag'd to many Greeks,
Even in the faith of valour, to appear
This morning to them.

Priam:
Ay, but thou shalt not go.

Hector:
> I must not break my faith.
> You know me dutiful; therefore, dear sir,
> Let me not shame respect, but give me leave
> To take that course by your consent and voice,
> Which you do here forbid me, royal Priam.

Cassandra:
> O Priam! yield not to him.

Andromache:
>   Do not, dear father.

Hector:
> Andromache, I am offended with you:
> Upon the love you bear me, get you in.
>   [*Exit Andromache*]

Troilus:
> This foolish, dreaming, superstitious girl
> Makes all these bodements.

Even as Cassandra has glimpsed the future she sees that Hector and Troilus are immovable and that Priam does not intend to restrain them. With her ally, 'Andromache, withdrawn, the "superstitious girl" sees the hopelessness of the situation.

Cassandra:
> O farewell! dear Hector.
> Look! how thou diest; look! how thy eye turns
>   pale;
> Look! how thy wounds do bleed at many vents:
> Hark! how Troy roars: how Hecuba cries out!
> How poor Andromache shrills her dolours forth!
> Behold, distraction, frenzy, and amazement,
> Like witless anticks, one another meet
> And all cry Hector! Hector's dead! O Hector!

Troilus:
> Away! Away!

Cassandra:
> Farewell. Yet, soft! Hector, I take my leave:
> Thou dost thyself and all our Troy deceive.
>> [*Exit.*

Hector:
> You are amaz'd, my liege, at her exclaim.
> Go in and cheer the town: we'll forth and fight;
> Do deeds worth praise and tell you them at night.

Priam:
> Farewell: the gods with safety stand about thee!

Cassandra's parting words are one of the best instances of clairvoyance in the Shakespeare tragedies. She is apparently seeing the death scene and what will occur in Troy when the news arrives. In Scene VIII, Act V, the final tragedy is enacted.

Hector:
> Most putrefied core, so fair without,
> Thy goodly armour thus hath cost thy life.
> Now is my day's work done; I'll take good
>> breath:
> Rest, sword; thou hast thy fill of blood and
>> death.
>> [*Puts off his helmet, and hangs his shield
>> behind him.*

>> *Enter Achilles and Myrmidons.*

Achilles:
> Look, Hector, how the sun begins to set;
> How ugly night comes breathing at his heels:
> Even with the vail and darking of the sun,
> To close the day up, Hector's life is done.

Hector:
> I am unarm'd; forego this vantage, Greek.

Achilles:
> Strike, fellows, strike! this is the man I seek.
>> [*Hector falls.*
> So, Ilion, fall thou next! now, Troy, sink down!

Here lies thy heart, thy sinews, and thy bone.
On! Myrmidons, and cry you all amain,
Achilles hath the mighty Hector slain.

THE WINTER'S TALE

The "oracle of Delphos" plays a very important part in the drama of *The Winter's Tale*. The insanely jealous king, Leontes, has ordered his innocent wife to prison and, notwithstanding the contrary opinion of everybody else, is so sure of the soundness of his groundless suspicions that he confidently sends two of the lords of his court to the oracle to there get a pronouncement upon the subject. In Scene I, Act II:

Leontes:

    Yet, for a greater confirmation,—
    For in an act of this importance 'twere
    Most piteous to be wild,—I have dispatch'd in
        post
    To sacred Delphos, to Apollo's temple,
    Cleomenes and Dion, whom you know
    Of stuff'd sufficiency. Now, from the oracle
    They will bring all; whose spiritual counsel had,
    Shall stop or spur me. Have I done well?

First Lord:

    Well done, my lord.

Leontes:

    Though I am satisfied and need no more
    Than what I know, yet shall the oracle
    Give rest to the minds of others, such as he
    Whose ignorant credulity will not
    Come up to the truth. So have we thought it
        good

> From our free person she should be confin'd,
> Lest that the treachery of the two fled hence
> Be left her to perform. Come, follow us:
> We are to speak in public; for this business
> Will raise us all.

Antigonus [*Aside*]:
> To laughter, as I take it,
> If the good truth were known.

Meantime he orders Antigonus to take the babe Perdita to some remote and desert place out of his dominions.

Leontes:
> To some remote and desart place quite out
> Of our dominions; and that there thou leave it,
> Without more mercy, to its own protection,
> And favour of the climate. As by strange fortune
> It came to us, I do in justice charge thee,
> On thy soul's peril and thy body's torture,
> That thou commend it strangely to some place,
> Where chance may nurse or end it.

Following this the two messengers entrusted with the mission to the oracle return. At the end of Act II we have this:

Servant:
> Please your highness, posts
> From those you sent to the oracle are come
> An hour since: Cleomenes and Dion,
> Being well arriv'd from Delphos, are both landed,
> Hasting to the court.

First Lord:
> So please you, sir, their speed
> Hath been beyond account.

Leontes:
> Twenty-three days
> They have been absent: 'tis good speed; foretells

The great Apollo suddenly will have
The truth of this appear. Prepare you, lords;
Summon a session, that we may arraign
Our most disloyal lady; for, as she hath
Been publicly accus'd, so shall she have
A just and open trial. While she lives
My heart will be a burden to me. Leave me,
And think upon my bidding.

The first scene in Act III is a seaport and the
returning lords, coming ashore, discuss in their
conversation the impressions received from the
country and the temple they have visited.

Enter Cleomenes and Dion.

Cleomenes:
    The climate's delicate, the air most sweet,
    Fertile the isle, the temple much surpassing
    The common praise it bears.
Dion:
                      I shall report,
    For most it caught me, the celestial habits,—
    Methinks I so should term them,—and the
        reverence
    Of the grave wearers. O, the sacrifice!
    How ceremonious, solemn, and unearthly
    It was i' the offering!
Cleomenes:
                      But of all, the burst
    And the ear-deafening voice o' the oracle,
    Kin to Jove's thunder, so surpris'd my sense,
    That I was nothing.
Dion:
                      If the event o' the journey
    Prove as successful to the queen,—O, be't so!—
    As it hath been to us rare, pleasant, speedy,
    The time is worth the use on't.
Cleomenes:
                      Great Apollo
    Turn all to the best! These proclamations,

> So forcing faults upon Hermione,
> I little like.
>
> *Dion:*
>
> The violent carriage of it
> Will clear or end the business: when the oracle,
> Thus by Apollo's great divine seal'd up,
> Shall the contents discover, something rare
> Even then will rush to knowledge.—Go:—fresh
> horses!
> And gracious to the issue!

When the queen was brought to trial, protesting her innocence, and being brutally arraigned by the king, the returning messengers reach the court with their important document:

> *Re-enter Officers, with Cleomenes and Dion.*
>
> *Officer:*
> You here shall swear upon this sword of justice,
> That you, Cleomenes and Dion, have
> Been both at Delphos, and from thence have
> brought
> This seal'd-up oracle, by the hand deliver'd
> Of great Apollo's priest, and that since then
> You have not dar'd to break the holy seal,
> Nor read the secrets in't.
>
> *Cleomenes and Dion:*
> All this we swear.
>
> *Leontes:*
> Break up the seals, and read.
>
> *Officer:*
> *Hermione is chaste; Polixenes blameless; Camillo a true subject; Leontes a jealous tyrant; his innocent babe truly begotten; and the king shall live without an heir if that which is lost be not found!*
>
> *Lords:*
> Now blessed be the great Apollo!
>
> *Hermione:*
> Praised!

Leontes:
    Hast thou read truth?
Officer:
                    Ay, my lord, even so
        As it is here set down.

"The king shall live without an heir if that which is lost be not found," refers, of course, to the babe cast away by Antigonus. The king's son being dead the lost child was the only living heir and for sixteen years the king believed himself to be without an heir; but the babe so cruelly abandoned had been found, reared in a shepherd's family and finally, by a combination of circumstances, was returned to her father's court.

The Winter's Tale also contains a most interesting dream. Antigonus himself relates it in Scene III, Act III, when, with a mariner to manage the boat, he took Perdita to a desert coast to be cast away.

Antigonus:
        Thou art perfect, then, our ship hath touch'd
            upon
        The desarts of Bohemia?
Mariner:
                    Ay, my lord; and fear
        We have landed in ill time; the skies look grimly
        And threaten present blusters. In my conscience,
        The heavens with what we have in hand are
            angry,
        And frown upon's.

Antigonus:
Their sacred wills be done! Go, get aboard;
Look to thy bark: I'll not be long before
I call upon thee.

Mariner:
Make your best haste, and go not
Too far i' the land: 'tis like to be loud weather;
Besides, this place is famous for the creatures
Of prey that keep upon't.

Antigonus:
Go thou away:
I'll follow instantly.

Mariner:
I am glad at heart
To be so rid of the business.   [*Exit.*

Antigonus:
Come, poor babe;
I have heard, but not believ'd, the spirits o' the
    dead
May walk again: if such thing be, thy mother
Appear'd to me last night, for ne'er was dream
So like a waking. To me comes a creature,
Sometimes her head on one side, some another;
I never saw a vessel of like sorrow,
So fill'd, and so becoming: in pure white robes,
Like very sanctity, she did approach
My cabin where I lay; thrice bow'd before me,
And, gasping to begin some speech, her eyes
Became two spouts: the fury spent, anon
Did this break from her: "Good Antigonus,
Since fate, against thy better disposition,
Hath made thy person for the thrower-out
Of my poor babe, according to thine oath,
Places remote enough are in Bohemia,
There weep and leave it crying; and, for the babe
Is counted lost forever, Perdita,
I prithee, call't: for this ungentle business,
Put on thee by my lord, thou ne'er shalt see
Thy wife Paulina more": and so, with shrieks,
She melted into air. Affrighted much
I did in time collect myself, and thought

This was so and no slumber. Dreams are toys;
Yet for this once, yea, superstitiously,
I will be squar'd by this. I do believe
Hermione hath suffer'd death; and that
Apollo would, this being indeed the issue
Of King Polixenes, it should here be laid,
Either for life or death, upon the earth
Of its right father. Blossom, speed thee well!
                    [*Laying down Child.*
There lie; and there thy character: there these;
                    [*Laying down a bundle.*
Which may, if fortune please, both breed thee,
    pretty,
And still rest thine. The storm begins: poor
    wretch!
That for thy mother's fault art thus exposed
To loss and what may follow. Weep I cannot,
But my heart bleeds, and most accurs'd am I
To be by oath enjoin'd to this. Farewell!

This dream is interesting in two points; it in-
duced Antigonus to leave the child where he
placed it, and there it was immediately found
and given a home. The dream makes an accurate forecast in the words "thou ne'er shalt see
thy wife Paulina more." Antigonus met a violent death within a few minutes after leaving
the abandoned babe. Many years later his wife
married Camillo.

SOOTHSAYERS AND PROPHECIES

It is King Richard himself who, in Scene II, Act IV, *King Richard III*, discloses the prophecy made to him in Ireland. Buckingham is insisting upon the fulfillment of the promised reward for his part in the enthronement of Richard and the latter is avoiding the point.

Buckingham:
>My lord, I claim the gift, my due by promise,
>For which your honour and your faith is pawn'd;
>The earldom of Hereford and the moveables
>Which you have promised I shall possess.

King Richard:
>Stanley, look to your wife: if she convey
>Letters to Richmond, you shall answer it.

Buckingham:
>What says your highness to my just request?

King Richard:
>I do remember me, Henry the Sixth
>Did prophesy that Richmond should be king;
>When Richmond was a little peevish boy.
>A king! perhaps—

Buckingham:
>My lord, your promise for the earldom—

King Richard:
>Richmond! When last I was at Exeter,
>The mayor in courtesy showed me the castle,
>And called it Rougemont: at which name I
>   started,

>Because a bard of Ireland told me once
>I should not live long after I saw Richmond.

There is a prophet in *King John* and he appears in Scene II, Act IV.   Philip Faulconbridge says:

>How I have sped among the clergymen,
>The sums I have collected shall express.
>But as I travell'd hither through the land,
>I find the people strangely fantasied,
>Possess'd with rumours, full of idle dreams,
>Not knowing what they fear, but full of fear.
>And here's a prophet that I brought with me
>From forth the streets of Pomfret, whom I found
>With many hundreds treading on his heels;
>To whom he sung, in rude harsh-sounding rimes,
>That, ere the next Ascension-day at noon,
>Your highness should deliver up your crown.

King John:
>Thou idle dreamer, wherefore didst thou so?

Peter:
>Foreknowing that the truth will fall out so.

King John:
>Hubert, away with him; imprison him:
>And on that day at noon, whereon, he says,
>I shall yield up my crown, let him be hang'd.

In Scene I, Act V, we have the confirmation of the prophecy.   John had found it necessary to compromise with the pope.   The text runs as follows:

King John:
>Thus have I yielded up into your hand
>The circle of my glory.

Pandulph [*Giving John the crown*]:
>   Take again
>From this my hand, as holding of the pope,
>Your sovereign greatness and authority.

King John:

    Now keep your holy word: go meet the French,
    And from his holiness use all your power
    To stop their marches 'fore we are inflam'd.
    Our discontented counties do revolt,
    Our people quarrel with obedience,
    Swearing allegiance and the love of soul
    To stranger blood, to foreign royalty.
    This inundation of mistemper'd humour
    Rests by you only to be qualified:
    Then pause not; for the present time's so sick,
    That present medicine must be minister'd,
    Or overthrow incurable ensues.

Pandulph:

    It was my breath that blew this tempest up
    Upon your stubborn usage of the pope;
    But since your are a gentle convertite,
    My tongue shall hush again this storm of war
    And make fair weather in your blustering land.
    On this Ascension-day, remember well,
    Upon your oath of service to the pope,
    Go I to make the French lay down their arms.

                                           [*Exit.*

King John:

    Is this Ascension-day? Did not the prophet
    Say that before Ascension-day at noon
    My crown I should give off? Even so I have:
    I did suppose it should be on constraint;
    But, heaven be thank'd, it is but voluntary.

When Henry VI found his fortunes declining
he saw the young earl of Richmond in the party
of noblemen in the tower (Scene VII, Act IV),
and laying a hand on the youth's head he says:

               * * * If secret powers
    Suggest but truth to my divining thoughts,
    This pretty lad will prove our country's bliss.
    His looks are full of peaceful majesty,
    His head by nature fram'd to wear a crown,

His hand to wield a sceptre, and himself
Likely in time to bless a regal throne.
Make much of him, my lords; for this is he
Must help you more than you are hurt by me.

After the king departed the Duke of Somerset says to the Earl of Oxford:

My lord, I like not of this flight of Edward's;
For doubtless Burgundy will yield him help,
And we shall have more wars before't be long.
As Henry's late presaging prophecy
Did glad my heart with hope of this young Rich-
    mond,
So doth my heart misgive me, in these conflicts
What may befall him to his harm and ours:
Therefore, Lord Oxford, to prevent the worst,
Forthwith we'll send him hence to Brittany,
Till storms be past of civil enmity.

It will be remembered that it was this youngster who afterward returned to England at the head of an army and, meeting King Richard, killed him in battle and then assumed the throne.

Cardinal Woolsey foretold the hour of his own death according to Griffith in Scene II, Act IV, *King Henry VIII.*

Queen Katharine had asked about the Cardinal's death and Griffith replied.

Katharine:
    Prithee, good Griffith, tell me how he died:
    If well, he stepp'd before me, happily,
    For my example.
Griffith:
            Well, the voice goes, madam:

For after the stout Earl Northumberland
Arrested him at York, and brought him forward,
As a man sorely tainted, to his answer,
He fell sick suddenly, and grew so ill
He could not sit his mule.

Katharine:

Alas! poor man.

Griffith:

At last, with easy roads, he came to Leicester;
Lodg'd in the abbey, where the reverend abbot,
With all his covent, honourably receiv'd him:
To whom he gave these words: 'O! father abbot,
An old man, broken with the storms of state,
Is come to lay his weary bones among ye;
Give him a little earth for charity.'
So went to bed, where eagerly his sickness
Pursu'd him still; and three nights after this,
About the hour of eight,—which he himself
Foretold should be his last,—full of repentance,
Continual meditations, tears, and sorrows,
He gave his honours to the world again,
His blessed part to heaven, and slept in peace.

War was on between Rome and Corioli when
Menenius announces, Scene I, Act II, *Coriol-
anus*:

The augurer tells me we shall have news to-night.

Later, in the same scene, Volumnia and Virginia bring confirmation:

Volumnia:

Honourable Menenius, my boy Marcius approaches; for the love of Juno, let's go.

Menenius:

Ha! Marcius coming home?

Volumnia:

Ay, worthy Menenius; and with most prosperous
approbation.

Menenius:
> Take my cap, Jupiter, and I thank thee. Hoo!
> Marcius coming home!

Volumnia and Virginia:
> Nay, 'tis true.

Volumnia:
> Look, here's a letter from him: the state hath
> another, his wife another; and, I think, there's
> one at home for you.

The occult interest in Antony and Cleopatra
lies wholly in the accurate prophecies of the
soothsayer. He appears in Scene II, Act I.
Charmian, Iras and Alexas, attendants on Cleopatra, enter:

Charmian:
> Lord Alexas, sweet Alexas, most any thing Alexas,
> almost most absolute Alexas, where's the sooth-
> sayer that you praised so to the queen? O! that
> I knew this husband, which, you say, must charge
> his horns with garlands.

Alexas:
> Soothsayer!

Soothsayer:
> Your will?

Charmian:
> Is this the man? Is't you, sir, that know things?

Soothsayer:
> In nature's infinite book of secrecy
> A little I can read.

Alexas:
> > Show him your hand.
> > *Enter Enobarbus.*

Enobarbus:
> Bring in the banquet quickly; wine enough
> Cleopatra's health to drink.

Charmian:
> Good sir, give me good fortune.

Soothsayer:
>I make not, but foresee.

Charmian:
>Pray then, foresee me one.

Soothsayer:
>You shall be yet far fairer than you are.

Charmian:
>He means in flesh.

Iras:
>No, you shall paint when you are old.

Charmian:
>Wrinkles forbid!

Alexas:
>Vex not his prescience; be attentive.

Charmian:
>Hush!

Soothsayer:
>You shall be more beloving than belov'd.

Charmian makes jests but Alexas enjoins her to listen farther to the soothsayer.

Soothsayer:
>You shall outlive the lady whom you serve.

Charmian:
>O excellent! I love long life better than figs.

Soothsayer:
>You have seen and prov'd a fairer former fortune
>Than that which is to approach.

Charmian continues to jest and scoff and asks the soothsayer "to tell Iras hers."

Soothsayer:
>Your fortunes are alike.

Iras:
>But how? but how? give me particulars.

Soothsayer:
>I have said.

Iras:
>Am I not an inch of fortune better than she?

Charmian:
    Well, if you were but an inch of fortune better
        than I, where would you choose it?
Iras:
    Not in my husband's nose.

Neither of the women take the matter seriously. Both talk mirthfully about it and have no thought of the approaching tragedy.

After the triumph of Octavius and the death of Antony, Cleopatra, Charmian and Iras are in the monument when the queen resolves upon death and the asps are smuggled past the guards under the pretense of bringing in figs. When Cleopatra makes her last farewell Iras falls and dies. After the death of the queen Charmian also applies an asp to her arm, is bitten and dies. Thus in every detail the soothsayer was verified. Charmian, as a favorite of the queen, had "seen fairer fortune" than that which was to approach. She outlived the lady whom she served by a few minutes. The fortunes of Charmian and Iras were alike, for they met the tragic fate of instant death at almost the same moment.

When Mark Antony returned to Rome and married Octavia he took the soothsayer along and the following conversation occurs in Caesar's house, in Scene III, Act II:

Antony:
    Now, sirrah; you do wish yourself in Egypt?

Soothsayer:
> Would I had never come from thence, nor you
> Thither!

Antony:
> If you can, your reason?

Soothsayer:
>   I see it in
> My motion, have it not in my tongue: but yet
> Hie you to Egypt again.

Antony:
>   Say to me,
> Whose fortunes shall rise higher, Caesar's or
>   mine?

Soothsayer:
> Caesar's.
> Therefore, O Antony! stay not by his side;
> Thy demon—that's thy spirit which keeps thee,—
>   is
> Noble, courageous, high, unmatchable,
> Where Caesar's is not; but near him thy angel
> Becomes a fear, as being o'erpower'd; therefore
> Make space enough between you.

Antony:
>   Speak this no more.

Soothsayer:
> To none but thee; no more but when to thee.
> If thou dost play with him at any game
> Thou art sure to lose, and, of that natural luck,
> He beats thee 'gainst the odds; thy lustre
>   thickens
> When he shines by. I say again, thy spirit
> Is all afraid to govern thee near him,
> But he away, 'tis noble.

Antony:
>   Get thee gone:
> Say to Ventidius I would speak with him.

After the soothsayer's exit, as above, Antony
soliloquizes upon what the seer had said:

Antony:
> He shall to Parthia. Be it art or hap
> He hath spoken true; the very dice obey him.
> And in our sports my better cunning faints
> Under his chance; if we draw lots he speeds,
> His cocks do win the battle still of mine
> When it is all to nought, and his quails ever
> Beat mine, inhoop'd, at odds.

The triumph of Caesar when the two armies met was sufficient confirmation of the soothsayer's delineation of the characters of Antony and Octavius Caesar. The cause of the former's defeat was clearly within himself.

The soothsayer who accompanied the Roman general Lucius, in *Cymbeline*, and was asked (Scene II, Act IV) for a forecast of the approaching battle replied:

> Last night the very gods show'd me a vision,—
> I fast and pray'd for their intelligence,—thus:
> I saw Jove's bird, the Roman eagle, wing'd
> From the spongy south to this part of the west,
> There vanish'd in the sunbeams; which portends,
> Unless my sins abuse my divination,
> Success to the Roman host.

In the early stages of the conflict the Romans rout the Britons and success seems certain for the invaders; but Leonatus, Valarius and the King's sons succeed in changing the retreat into unexpected victory. When the Roman prisoners, including the general and soothsayer, are brought before Cymbeline and he condemns

them to death, it seems that the prediction of
Roman success had been far from the facts. A
sudden turn of affairs, however, which nobody
could have foreseen, restored to the King his
sons and daughter and gave life and liberty to
the prisoners. Cymbeline, learning of the per-
fidy of the dead Queen, was quick to acknowl-
edge that he was in the wrong, and although the
Britons had won the day, he renounced any ad-
vantage that came with success (Scene V, Act
V):

> And, Caius Lucius,
> Although the victor, we submit to Caesar,
> And to the Roman empire, promising
> To pay our wonted tribute, from the which
> We were dissuaded by our wicked queen;
> Whom heavens—in justice both on her and hers—
> Have laid most heavy hand.

Soothsayer:

> The fingers of the powers above do tune
> The harmony of this peace. The vision
> Which I made known to Lucius ere the stroke
> Of this yet scarce-cold battle, at this instant
> Is full accomplish'd; for the Roman eagle,
> From south to west on wing soaring aloft,
> Lessen'd herself, and in the beams o' the sun
> So vanish'd: which foreshadow'd our princely
>   eagle,
> The imperial Caesar, should again unite
> His favour with the radiant Cymbeline,
> Which shines here in the west.

ASTROLOGY

The references in various plays to astrology are interesting not only to the student of the occult but also as showing how commonly astrological expressions were employed in Shakespeare's day.

In Scene II, Act V, *Much Ado About Nothing*, Benedick says of his inability to write well:

> I was not born under a riming planet,
> Nor I cannot woo in festival terms.

Don John, in that play, remonstrates with Conrade for his lack of a philosophical view of human nature and his failure to understand why he, Don John, is sad without present cause for it:

> I wonder that thou, being—as thou say'st thou art—born under Saturn, goest about to apply a moral medicine to a mortifying mischief. I cannot hide what I am.

When the Duke in *Twelfth Night* sends Viola on the courting mission to Olivia he remarks:

> I know thy constellation is right apt
> For this affair.

In that distressing scene in *The Winter's Tale* in which the king gives way to blind rage on account of his groundless jealousy and orders the queen to prison, she protests her innocence and then adds with patient resignation:

> There's some ill planet reigns:
> I must be patient till the heavens look
> With an aspect more favourable.

When Richard the Third is proposing to Queen Elizabeth, widow of his brother Edward, that her daughter Elizabeth marry him and is hypo-critically swearing that he loves her daughter, he says:

> Heaven and fortune bar me happy hours!
> Day, yield me not thy light; nor, night, thy rest!
> Be opposite all planets of good luck
> To my proceeding, if, with pure heart's love,
> Immaculate devotion, holy thoughts,
> I tender not thy beauteous princely daughter!

Reminded that he is the murderer of her brothers, he excuses himself with

> Lo! at their births good stars were opposite!

In Scene II, Act I, *Julius Caesar*, Cassius says:

> Men at some time are masters of their fates:
> The fault, dear Brutus, is not in our stars,
> But in ourselves, that we are underlings.

Warwick says to King Henry, Scene VI, Act IV, *Third Part of King Henry VI*:

> Your Grace hath still been famed for virtuous;
> And now may seem as wise as virtuous,
> By spying and avoiding Fortune's malice;
> For few men rightly temper with the stars:
> Yet in this one thing let me blame your Grace,
> For choosing me when Clarence is in place.

To which the duke replies:

> No, Warwick, thou art worthy of the sway,
> To whom the heavens, in thy nativity
> Adjudg'd an olive branch and laurel crown,
> As likely to be blessed in peace, and war.

A speech by Ulysses in Scene III, Act I, *Troilus and Cressida*, contains the following:

> The heavens themselves, the planets, and this
>   centre
> Observe degree, priority, and place,
> Insisture, course, proportion, season, form,
> Office and custom, in all line of order:
> And therefore is the glorious planet Sol
> In noble eminence enthron'd and spher'd
> Amidst the other; whose med'cinable eye
> Corrects the ill aspects of planets evil,
> And posts, like the commandment of a king,
> Sans check, to good and bad: but when the
>   planets
> In evil mixture to disorder wander,
> What plagues, and what portents, what mutiny,
> What raging of the sea, shaking of earth,
> Commotion in the winds, frights, changes, horrors,
> Divert and crack, rend and deracinate
> The unity and married calm of states
> Quite from their fixture!

The first words spoken in the *First Part of King Henry VI* are by the Duke of Bedford:

> Hung be the heavens with black, yield day to
>   night!
> Comets, importing change of times and states,
> Brandish your crystal tresses in the sky,
> And with them scourge the bad revolting stars,
> That have consented unto Henry's death!

In the same scene the Duke of Exeter exclaims:

> What! shall we curse the planets of mishap
> That plotted thus our glory's overthrow?

Prospero, the adept, in Scene II, Act I, *The Tempest*, speaks thus:

> By accident most strange, bountiful Fortune,
> Now my dear lady, hath mine enemies
> Brought to this shore; and by my prescience
> I find my zenith doth depend upon
> A most auspicious star, whose influence
> If now I court not but omit, my fortunes
> Will ever after droop.

Just before the two Talbots were slain in the *First Part of King Henry VI*, Lord Talbot says to his son in Scene V, Act IV:

> O young John Talbot! I did send for thee
> To tutor thee in strategems of war,
> That Talbot's name might be in thee reviv'd
> When sapless age, and weak unable limbs
> Should bring thy father to his drooping chair.
> But,—O malignant and ill-boding stars!
> Now thou art come unto a feast of death,

A terrible and unavoided danger:
Therefore, dear boy, mount on my swiftest horse,
And I'll direct thee how thou shalt escape
By sudden flight: come, dally not, be gone.

When Mark Antony, in the rage of defeat, seized the messenger from Octavius Caesar and ordered him whipped, Scene XI, Act III, he says of Octavius:

> * * * For he seems
> Proud and disdainful, harping on what I am,
> Not what he knew I was: he makes me angry;
> And at this time most easy 'tis to do't,
> When my good stars, that were my former guides,
> Have empty left their orbs, and shot their fires
> Into the abysm of hell.

In Scene I, Act V, Octavius scliloquizes on the fate of Antony:

> O Antony!
> I have follow'd thee to this; but we do lance
> Diseases in our bodies: I must perforce
> Have shown to thee such a declining day,
> Or look on thine; we could not stall together
> In the whole world. But yet let me lament,
> With tears as sovereign as the blood of hearts,
> That thou, my brother, my competitor
> In top of all design, my mate in empire,
> Friend and companion in the front of war,
> The arm of mine own body, and the heart
> Where mine his thoughts did kindle, that our
>   stars,
> Unreconciliable, should divide
> Our equalness to this.

Autolycus, the thieving rogue, in *The Winter's Tale,* says of himself in Scene II, Act IV:

My father named me Autolycus; who being, as I am, littered under Mercury, was likewise a snapper-up of unconsidered trifles.

CEREMONIAL MAGIC

In the *Second Part of King Henry VI* a correct forecast of the fate of three prominent persons is obtained by ceremonial magic in which Margery Jourdain, a witch or medium, and Bolingbroke, a conjurer, are the chief actors.

In Scene II, Act I, the Duchess of Gloucester, ambitious and jealous of those who rank above her, is plotting with Hume.

Duchess:
> What sayst thou, man? hast thou as yet conferr'd
> With Margery Jourdain, the cunning witch,
> With Roger Bolingbroke, the conjurer?
> And will they undertake to do me good?

Hume:
> This they have promised, to show your highness
> A spirit rais'd from depth of underground,
> That shall make answer to such questions
> As by your Grace shall be propounded him.

Duchess:
> It is enough: I'll think upon the questions.
> When from St. Alban's we do make return
> We'll see these things effected to·the full.
> Here, Hume, take this reward; make merry, man,
> With thy confed'rates in this weighty cause.

It is in Scene IV, in the duke's garden, that the sequel follows:

Hume:
> Come, my masters; the duchess, I tell you, expects performance of your promises.

Bolingbroke:
> Master Hume, we are therefore provided. Will her ladyship behold and hear our exorcisms?

Hume:
> Ay; what else? fear you not her courage.

Bolingbroke:
> I have heard her reported to be a woman of invincible spirit: but it shall be convenient, Master Hume, that you be by her aloft while we be busy below; and so, I pray you, go in God's name, and leave us. [*Exit Hume.*] Mother Jourdain, be you prostrate, and grovel on the earth; John Southwell, read you; and let us to our work.
>   *Enter Duchess aloft, Hume following.*

Duchess:
> Well said, my masters, and welcome all.
> To this gear the sooner the better.

Bolingbroke:
> Patience, good lady; wizards know their times:
> Deep night, dark night, the silent of the night,
> The time of the night when Troy was set on fire;
> The time when screech-owls cry, and ban-dogs howl,
> And spirits walk, and ghosts break up their graves,
> That time best fits the work we have in hand.
> Madam, sit you, and fear not: whom we raise
> We will make fast within a hallow'd verge.
>   [*Here they perform the ceremonies belonging, and make the circle; Bolingbroke, or Southwell reads, Conjuro te, etc. It thunders and lightens terribly; then the spirit riseth.*]

Spirit:
> Adsum.

M. Jourdain:
> Asmath!
> By the eternal God, whose name and power

Thou tremblest at, answer that I shall ask,
For till thou speak, thou shalt not pass from
    hence.
Spirit:
Ask what thou wilt. That I had said and done!
Bolingbroke:
First, of the king: what shall of him become?
Spirit:
The Duke yet lives that Henry shall depose;
But him outlive, and die a violent death.
  [*As the spirit speaks, Southwell writes the answers.*
Bolingbroke:
What fate awaits the Duke of Suffolk?
Spirit:
By water shall he die and take his end.
Bolingbroke:
What shall befall the Duke of Somerset?
Spirit:
Let him shun castles:
Safer shall he be upon the sandy plains
Than where castles mounted stand.
Have done, for more I hardly can endure.

As the play develops each one of these prophecies is found to be true to the facts. Henry VI is deposed by Richard Plantagenet, Duke of York (Scene I, Act I, *Third Part of King Henry VI*) but the duke is soon afterward slain on the battle field. In Scene VI, Act V, Richard, afterwards Duke of Gloucester, enters London Tower and assassinates King Henry. Thus he was deposed by a duke but outlived the duke and finally met violent death.

After the Duke of Suffolk had accomplished the cruel death of King Henry's uncle, Duke

Humphrey, and was banished by the king, he sought to leave the country in disguise and was captured with others who were permitted to offer ransom for their lives. But a sterner fate was in store for Suffolk. In Scene I, Act IV, *Second Part of King Henry VI*, we have this:

Whitmore:
 I lost mine eye in laying the prize aboard,
 [*To Suffolk*]:
 And therefore to avenge it shalt thou die;
 And so should these if I might have my will.
Captain:
 Be not so rash: take ransom; let him live.
Suffolk:
 Look on my George; I am a gentleman:
 Rate me at what thou wilt, thou shalt be paid.
Whitmore:
 And so am I; my name is Walter Whitmore.
 How now! why start'st thou? what! doth **death** affright?
Suffolk:
 Thy name affrights me, in whose sound is death.
 A cunning man did calculate my birth,
 And told me that by *Water* I should die:
 Yet let not this make thee be bloody-minded;
 Thy name is—*Gaultier*, being rightly sounded.
Whitmore:
 Gaultier, or *Walter*, which it is I care not;
 Never yet did base dishonour blur our name
 But with our sword we wip'd away the blot:
 Therefore, when merchant-like I sell revenge,
 Broke be my sword, my arms torn and defac'd,
 And I proclaim'd a coward through the world!
       [*Lays hold on Suffolk.*
Suffolk:
 Stay, Whitmore; for thy prisoner is a prince,
 The Duke of Suffolk, William de la Pole.

Whitmore:
> The Duke of Suffolk muffled up in rags!

But the disclosure of his identity only made his death more certain for the Captain then commended Whitmore's decision:

Captain:
> Convey him hence, and on our longboat's side
> Strike off his head.

The Duke of Somerset met his fate in battle, Scene II, Act V:

> *Enter Richard and Somerset, fighting;*
> *Somerset is killed.*

Richard:
> So, lie thou there;
> For underneath an alehouse' paltry sign,
> The Castle in Saint Alban's, Somerset
> Hath made the wizard famous in his death.

There can be no mistaking the accuracy of the prophecy thus fulfilled. "Castles mounted" is a very definite reference to the signboard of the "Castle in Saint Alban's," under which he died.

The ceremonial magic in Scene I, Act I, and in Scene I, Act IV, *Macbeth*, is the most dramatic that occurs in the Shakespeare plays and has been referred to in the chapter on *Macbeth*.

Aside from the ceremonial magic performed by the witches in *Macbeth*, the spirits that appear for Joan of Arc and for the conspirators in *The Second Part of King Henry VI*, there is another notable instance. In *The First Part of King Henry IV*, Hotspur, Worcester, Mortimer and Glendower are discussing their plans when Glendower makes assertions about himself which Hotspur receives with humorous incredulity, Act III, Scene I:

Glendower:
> No, here it is.
> Sit, cousin Percy; sit, good cousin Hotspur;
> For by that name as oft as Lancaster
> Doth speak of you, his cheek looks pale and with
> A rising sigh he wishes you in heaven.

Hotspur:
> And you in hell, as often as he hears
> Owen Glendower spoke of.

Glendower:
> I cannot blame him: at my nativity
> The front of heaven was full of fiery shapes,
> Of burning cressets; and at my birth
> The frame and huge foundation of the earth
> Shak'd like a coward.

Hotspur:
> Why, so it would have done at the same season,
> if your mother's cat had but kittened, though
> yourself had never been born.

Glendower:
> I say the earth did shake when I was born.

Hotspur:
> And I say the earth was not of my mind,
> If you suppose as fearing you it shook.

Glendower:
> The heavens were all on fire, the earth did
>   tremble.

Hotspur:
> O! then the earth shook to see the heavens on
>   fire,
> And not in fear of your nativity.

Diseased nature oftentimes breaks forth
In strange eruptions; oft the teeming earth
Is with a kind of colic pinch'd and vex'd
By the imprisoning of unruly wind
Within her womb; which, for enlargement striv-
    ing,
Shakes the old beldam earth, and topples down
Steeples and moss-grown towers. At your birth
Our grandam earth, having this distemperature,
In passion shook.

Glendower:

               Cousin, of many men
I do not bear these crossings. Give me leave
To tell you once again that at my birth
The front of heaven was full of fiery shapes,
The goats ran from the mountains, and the herds
Were strangely clamorous to the frighted fields.
These signs have marked me extraordinary;
And all the courses of my life do show
I am not in the roll of common men.
Where is he living, clipp'd in with the sea
That chides the banks of England, Scotland,
    Wales,
Which calls me pupil, or hath read to me?
And bring him out that is but woman's son
Can trace me in the tedious ways of art
And hold me pace in deep experiments.

Hotspur:

I think there's no man speaks better Welsh.
I'll to dinner.

Mortimer:

Peace, cousin Percy! you will make him mad.

Glendower:

I can call spirits from the vasty deep.

Hotspur:

Why, so can I, or so can any man;
   But will they come when you do call for them?

Glendower:

Why, I can teach thee, cousin, to command
The devil.

Hotspur:
>   And I can teach thee, coz, to shame the devil
>   By telling truth: tell truth and shame the devil.
>   If thou have power to raise him, bring him
>   hither,
>   And I'll be sworn I have power to shame him
>   hence.
>   O! while you live, tell truth and shame the devil!

A little later it is proposed that Lady Mortimer sing and at this point Glendower makes good his boast.

Glendower:
>   Do so;
>   And those musicians that shall play to you
>   Hang in the air a thousand leagues from hence,
>   And straight they shall be here: sit, and attend.
>   [*Glendower speaks some Welsh words, and
>   music is heard.*

Hotspur:
>   Now I perceive the devil understands Welsh;
>   And 'tis no marvel he is so humorous.
>   By'r lady, he's a good musician.

JOAN OF ARC

Joan of Arc is represented in the *First Part of King Henry VI* as a sorceress and as having superphysical powers. In Scene II, Act I, the attempt by the French army to raise the siege of Orleans has been abandoned after a consultation following an attack; but at that moment the Dauphin's ally appears and introduces a new factor:

> Methinks your looks are sad, your cheer appall'd:
> Hath the late overthrow wrought this offence?
> Be not dismay'd, for succour is at hand:
> A holy maid hither with me I bring,
> Which by a vision sent to her from heaven
> Ordained is to raise this tedious siege,
> And drive the English forth the bounds of France.
> The spirit of deep prophecy she hath,
> Exceeding the nine sibyls of old Rome;
> What's past and what's to come she can descry.
> Speak, shall I call her in? Believe my words,
> For they are certain and infallible.

The Dauphin orders her called in and before she comes arranges a little trap for her.

> * * * But first, to try her skill,
> Reignier, stand thou as Dauphin in my place:
> Question her proudly; let thy looks be stern:
> By this means shall we sound what skill she hath.

The Dauphin retires behind the curtains and Joan of Arc is brought in. Reignier, pretending to be the Dauphin, says:

> Fair maid, is't thou wilt do these wondrous feats?

Joan:

> Reignier, is't thou that thinkest to beguile me?
> Where is the Dauphin? Come, come from be-
>   hind;
> I know thee well, though never seen before.
> Be not amaz'd, there's nothing hid from me:
> In private will I talk with thee apart.
> Stand back, you lords, and give us leave a while.

Reignier:

> She takes upon her bravely at first dash.

Joan:

> Dauphin, I am by birth a shepherd's daughter,
> My wit untrain'd in any kind of art.
> Heaven and our Lady gracious hath it pleas'd
> To shine on my contemptible estate:
> Lo! whilst I waited on my tender lambs,
> And to sun's parching heat display'd my cheeks,
> God's mother deigned to appear to me,
> And in a vision full of majesty
> Will'd me to leave my base vocation
> And free my country from calamity:
> Her aid she promis'd and assur'd success;
> In complete glory she reveal'd herself;
> And, whereas I was black and swart before,
> With those clear rays which she infus'd on me,
> That beauty am I bless'd with which you see.
> Ask me what questions thou canst possible
> And I will answer unpremeditated:
> My courage try by combat, if thou dar'st,
> And thou shalt find that I exceed my sex.
> Resolve on this, thou shalt be fortunate
> If thou receive me for thy war-like mate.

Charles:

> Thou hast astonish'd me with thy high terms.

Only this proof I'll of thy valour make,
In single combat thou shalt buckle with me,
And if thou vanquishest, thy words are true;
Otherwise I renounce all confidence.

Joan:

I am prepar'd: here is my keen-edg'd sword.
Deck'd with five flower-de-luces on each side;
The which at Touraine, in Saint Katharine's
    churchyard,
Out of a great deal of old iron I chose forth.

Charles:

Then come, o' God's name: I fear no woman.

Joan:

And, while I live, I'll never fly from a man.
    [*They fight, and Joan La Pucelle overcomes.*

Charles:

Stay, stay thy hands! thou art an Amazon,
And fightest with the sword of Deborah.

A little later Joan of Arc says:

Assign'd am I to be the English scourge.
This night the siege assuredly I'll raise:
Expect Saint Martin's summer, halcyon days,
Since I have entered into these wars.
Glory is like a circle in the water,
Which never ceaseth to enlarge itself,
Till by broad spreading it disperse to nought.
With Henry's death the English circle ends;
Dispersed are the glorys it included.
Now am I like that proud insulting ship
Which Caesar and his fortune bare at once.

Charles:

Was Mahomet inspired with a dove?
Thou with an eagle art inspired then.
Helen, the mother of great Constantine,
Nor yet Saint Philip's daughters were like thee.
Bright star of Venus, fall'n down on the earth,
How may I reverently worship thee enough?

Alencon:
　　Leave off delays and let us raise the siege.
Reignier:
　　Woman, do what thou canst to save our honours;
　　Drive them from Orleans and be immortalis'd.

It is in Scene IV, Act I, that old Talbot, having been released through an exchange of prisoners, is welcomed back; and in which Salisbury, his close friend, is killed. Talbot is the most fearless warrior of the invading hosts and his ferocity is brought out by the conversation.

Salisbury:
　　Yet tell'st thou not how thou wert entertain'd.
Talbot:
　　With scoffs and scorns and contumelious taunts.
　　In open market-place produc'd they me,
　　To be a public spectacle to all:
　　Here, said they, is the terror of the French,
　　The scarecrow that affrights our children so.
　　Then broke I from the officers that led me,
　　And with my nails digg'd stones out of the
　　　　ground
　　To hurl at the beholders of my shame.
　　My grisly countenance made others fly.
　　None durst come near for fear of sudden death.
　　In iron walls they deem'd me not secure;
　　So great fear of my name 'mongst them was
　　　　spread
　　That they suppos'd I could rend bars of steel
　　And spurn in pieces posts of adamant:
　　Wherefore a guard of chosen shot I had,
　　That walk'd about me every minute-while;
　　And if I did but stir out of my bed
　　Ready they were to shoot me to the heart.

Notwithstanding Talbot's great valor and the

fact that he has just sworn vengeance on the French for the death of Salisbury, he is not able to vanquish Joan. In Scene V, Act I, we have this:

Talbot:

Where is my strength, my valour, and my force?
Our English troops retire, I cannot stay them;
A woman clad in armor chaseth them;
   Re-enter Joan La Pucelle.
Here, here she comes. I'll have a bout with thee:
Devil, or devil's dam, I'll conjure thee:
Blood will I draw on thee, thou art a witch,
And straightway give thy soul to him thou serv'st.

Joan:

Come, come; 'tis only I that must disgrace thee.
         [They fight.

Talbot:

Heavens, can you suffer hell so to prevail?
My breast I'll burst with straining of my courage,
And from my shoulders crack my arms asunder,
But I will chastise this high-minded strumpet.
        [They fight again.

Joan:

Talbot, farewell; thy hour is not yet come;
I must go victual Orleans forthwith.
 [A short alarum; then La Pucelle enters the
        town with soldiers.
O'ertake me if thou canst; I scorn thy strength.
Go, go, cheer up thy hunger-starved men;
Help Salisbury to make his testament:
This day is ours, as many more shall be. *[Exit.*

Talbot:

My thoughts are whirled like a potter's wheel;
I know not where I am, nor what I do;
A witch, by fear, not force, like Hannibal,
Drives back our troops and conquers as she lists:
So bees with smoke, and doves with noisome
 stench,

Are from their hives and houses driven away.
They called us for our fierceness English dogs;
Now, like to whelps, we crying run away.
                    [*A short alarum.*
Hark, countrymen! either renew the fight,
Or tear the lions out of England's coat;
Renounce your soil, give sheep in lions' stead:
Sheep run not half so treacherous from the wolf,
Or horse or oxen from the leopard,
As you fly from your oft-subdued slaves.
                [*Alarum. Another skirmish.*
It will not be: retire into your trenches:
You all consented unto Salisbury's death,
For none would strike a stroke in his revenge.
Pucelle is entered into Orleans
In spite of us or aught that we could do.
O! would I were to die with Salisbury.
The shame hereof will make me hide my head.
            [*Alarum. Retreat. Exeunt Talbot and his
                                        forces, etc.*

After the retaking of Roan by the English,
Joan proposes the strategy of separating the
Duke of Burgundy from the English army and
is successful. This occurs in Scene III, Act III.

Charles:
    A parley with the Duke of Burgundy!

Burgundy:
    Who craves a parley with the Burgundy?

Joan:
    The princely Charles of France, thy countryman.

Burgundy:
    What sayst thou, Charles? for I am marching
        hence.

Charles:
    Speak, Pucelle, and enchant him with thy words.

Joan:

> Brave Burgundy, undoubted hope of France!
> Stay, let thy humble handmaid speak to thee.

Burgundy:

> Speak on; but be not over-tedious.

Joan:

> Look on thy country, look on fertile France,
> And see the cities and the towns defac'd
> By wasting ruin of the cruel foe.
> As looks the mother on her lowly babe
> When death doth close his tender dying eyes,
> See, see the pining malady of France;
> Behold the wounds, the most unnatural wounds,
> Which thou thyself hast giv'n her woeful breast.
> O! turn thy edged sword another way;
> Strike those that hurt, and hurt not those that
> help.
> One drop of blood drawn from thy country's
> bosom,
> Should grieve thee more than streams of foreign
> gore:
> Return thee therefore, with a flood of tears,
> And wash away thy country's stained spots.

Burgundy:

> Either she hath bewitch'd me with her words,
> Or nature makes me suddenly relent.

Joan:

> Besides, all French and France exclaims on thee,
> Doubting thy birth and lawful progeny.
> Who join'st thou with but with a lordly nation
> That will not trust thee but for profit's sake?
> When Talbot hath set footing once in France,
> And fashion'd thee that instrument of ill,
> Who then but English Henry will be lord,
> And thou be thrust out like a fugitive?
> Call we to mind, and mark but this for proof,
> Was not the Duke of Orleans thy foe,
> And was he not in England prisoner?
> But when they heard he was thine enemy,
> They set him free, without his ransom paid,

> In spite of Burgundy and all his friends.
> See then, thou fight'st against thy countrymen!
> And join'st with them will be thy slaughter-men.
> Come, come, return; return thou wand'ring lord;
> Charles and the rest will take thee in their arms.

Burgundy:
> I am vanquished; these haughty words of hers
> Have batter'd me like roaring cannon-shot,
> And made me almost yield upon my knees.
> Forgive me, country, and sweet countrymen!
> And, lords, accept this hearty kind embrace:
> My forces and my power of men are yours.

Later, when the tide of war once more sets against France, Joan of Arc invokes help from intangible realms. In Scene III, Act V, she says:

> The regent conquers and the Frenchmen fly.
> Now help, ye charming spells and periapts;
> And ye choice spirits that admonish me
> And give me signs of future accidents:
>   [*Thunder.*
> You speedy helpers, that are substitutes
> Under the lordly monarch of the north,
> Appear, and aid me in this enterprise!

The spirits appear, walk silently, and finally, to her impatient appeal, shake their heads and depart. She continues:

> See! they forsake me. Now the time is come,
> That France must vail her lofty-plumed crest,
> And let her head fall into England's lap.
> My ancient incantations are too weak,

And hell too strong for me to buckle with:
Now, France, thy glory droopeth to the dust.

It is immediately after this that she is taken
prisoner and sent to the stake.

THE FAIRIES

In two of the Shakespeare plays, fairies take an important part. The skepticism of the twentieth century has scornfully rejected the serious views of the world in ancient days on the subject of fairies but apparently the time is near when ocular evidence will demonstrate their reality. Those who have read *The Coming of The Fairies* by A. Conan Doyle, will be familiar with the story of how some of them were photographed in a glen in the North of England and of the array of expert opinion on the genuineness of the negatives. The subject will doubtless be in controversy for a few years until the evidence becomes so abundant that incredulity must give way. Meantime, an examination of that rollicking comedy, *A Midsummer-Night's Dream*, and the drama of *The Tempest*, will furnish interesting descriptions of the fairies.

Just as the great dramatist takes clairvoyance, premonitions and ghosts as facts of nature, he presents the fairies likewise. They are realities and in *The Tempest* the number of charac-

ters on the stage is about equally divided between human beings and fairies.

In *A Midsummer-Night's Dream* the curtain
that shuts a large part of nature from the vision
of most of us is lifted a little and we get a
glimpse of the life that cannot be observed with
the physical senses. The fairies dance and frolic
for us and, while the poet avails himself of the
license to which the muse is rightly entitled, he
gives us a faithful portrayal of the characteristics of these witching denizens of the world invisible. In their essentials there is no difference
between the fairies of the Shakespeare plays and
the nature spirits of the Leadbeater books. Puck
makes himself visible or invisible at will and
quickly assumes various forms to suit the purpose of the moment; and he greatly enjoys the
task Oberon assigns him of misleading and
glamouring mortals—a characteristic familiar to
students of the astral and etheric regions.

> I'll follow you, I'll lead you 'bout around,
> Through bog, through bush, through brake,
>   through briar:
> Sometimes a horse, I'll be, sometimes a hound,
> A hog, a headless bear, sometimes a fire;
> And neigh, and bark, and grunt, and roar, and
>   burn,
> Like horse, hound, hog, bear, fire, at every turn.

The dramatist lets us see that these non-

human but intelligent beings belong to another
order of creation and do not understand life as
we do. A thing of much value to us has no
value in their eyes. They would not exchange
a knowledge of the favorite spots in which

> To dance our ringlets to the whistling wind,

for all the wealth and joys of mortals; and looking on at the incomprehensible actions of the
physical plane people Puck exclaims,

> Lord, what fools these mortals be!

C. W. Leadbeater, in his work *The Astral
Plane*, describes these nature spirits—as the
whole of this great lower strata of the deva evolution is known to Theosophy—as "tricky and
mischievous but rarely malicious." These
characteristics come out prominently in such
characters as Puck and Ariel. Puck describes
himself as "that merry wanderer of the night"
who devotes himself with great gusto to good-
natured mischief, for his own and others' entertainment, and it was when he was playing his
favorite tricks on his victims that they would
"swear a merrier hour was never wasted." Ariel,
in *The Tempest*, takes similar delight in making
a victim of Caliban. He finds Caliban, on account of his ignorance and stupidity, easily

frightened and Ariel plays all manner of pranks with him, leading him astray into bogs, suddenly assuming the form of a porcupine, of which Caliban had great dread, and again appearing in his pathway as a chattering ape to the terror of Caliban and the amusement of Ariel. How true to nature this character is drawn may be seen from the description of the author and investigator above quoted. Referring to the characteristics of this class of astral entities he says:

"In most cases when they come in contact with man they either show indifference or dislike, or else take an impish delight in deceiving him and playing childish tricks upon him. * * * They are greatly assisted in their tricks by the wonderful power which they possess of casting a glamour over those who yield themselves to their influence, so that such victims for the time see and hear only what these fairies impress upon them, exactly as the mesmerized subject sees, hears, feels and believes whatever the magnetizer wishes."—*The Astral Plane*, p. **79**.

Those who credit the existence of fairies at all, are likely to think of them as a little group of beings exhibiting no great diversity of form or powers. The student of occultism knows what a misconception this is, and here again the great

dramatist sets us right both in *The Tempest* and
in *A Midsummer-Night's Dream*. The dislike
of these nature spirits for the cities and their
love of the secluded places, commented upon in
The Astral Plane, also comes out clearly in these
two plays.

It is an interesting fact that those Shakespeare plays which the critics are generally
agreed upon as being the greatest of them all
are those which contain the most occultism. No
other play ever written, say the critics, has received such universal praise as *The Tempest*. It
was the last dramatic work of the poet's life and
in it is seen, according to general opinion, the
acme of his matchless art. Now *The Tempest*,
of all the plays, is the most occult. As would
be expected there is much difference of opinion
about its purpose but none about its merit. To
its analysis learned minds have given the most
painstaking labor and it is the theme of many
a weighty volume. To the student of occultism
this play and *A Midsummer-Night's Dream* are
companions and constitute a class in the Shakespeare plays. The opinions about them, and
particularly about *The Tempest*, are almost as
numerous as the critics; but perhaps nobody is
better qualified to interpret such literature than

Victor Hugo. Of these two plays he says: "*A Midsummer-Night's Dream* depicts the action of the invisible world on man; *The Tempest* symbolizes the action of man on the invisible world."

Prospero is the central figure in *The Tempest* and in him we have a picture of the adept, controlling the lower orders of life in the invisible world and through that power controlling in perfect mastery the elements. He is the white magician. He is omnipotent but uses his power only for righteous ends and always with mercy. He sometimes temporarily assumes an apparent harshness but is always in fact the personification of gentleness and no offense is too serious for him to forgive and forget. He returns good for evil, and hardship is brought upon the wrong-doers only for the purpose of bringing the arrogant and conscienceless to their senses. He has clairvoyant vision and moves about in his astral body; for he is not merely aware of what is occurring at a distance but is represented as being *invisibly present* when Ariel arraigns the three evil-doers for their misdeeds. He knows of the danger that threatens the king and Gonzalo and sends Ariel to prevent the would-be assassins from murdering them by awakening

Gonzalo at the right instant. He has the power
to instantly hypnotize Ferdinand and disarm
him with a stick when he draws his sword. To
the invisibles that serve him Prospero issues
positive commands and exacts unquestioning
obedience. Fleming says of this character that
Prospero is the personification of wisdom, of
power that can execute justice, rewarding right
and circumventing wrong.

It was through control of the nature spirits
that Prospero produced the storm at sea that
drove the ship containing his treacherous brother
and his allies to the island shore; and it was
through his command of the same entities that
his farther plans were successfully executed.
Ariel, the chief of the invisible hosts that serve
Prospero, not any too willingly, is visible or
invisible at pleasure and instantaneously assumes various forms at will. He possesses the
power of glamour in remarkable degree and the
shipwrecked men are fully persuaded that the
vessel is lost. Ariel reports to Prospero that
"the ship, though invisible to them, is safe in the
harbor." He separates the stranded men and
each group or individual believes all others are
lost. The king believes his son is dead while
the prince is certain his father has perished; and

through the state of mind thus brought about the problem in hand is worked out successfully. In working them up into the condition that finally made them tractable and penitent, Ariel, in the form of a harpy, frightened the king, Sebastian and Antonio — "three men of sin" — nearly out of their wits. Again, at the head of a band of the denizens of the world invisible, who take visible form, he drives the marauders and would-be murderers from Prospero's home. The final task assigned him by Prospero is to carry out the magician's promise to the king that on the return voyage he shall have "calm seas," and "auspicious gales." With the execution of this task Ariel gained his longed-for freedom from serving the magician whom he called "great master" and won the life he much preferred:

> Merrily, merrily shall I live now
> Under the blossom that hangs on the bough.

Prospero's compassion is as great as his power. He addresses the would-be assassins as "my friends" and says "let us not remember our troubles past."

Prospero is an adept but not a "Master of Wisdom." His occult power is temporary. He renounces it after he regains his dukedom and returns to material affairs. Like Bulwer Lytton, who also utilized his knowledge of occultism in writing some of his novels, Shakespeare uses his remarkably accurate knowledge of the hidden side of nature in constructing many of the plays; but while he exercises an author's license in adapting material to the story in hand, he is always meticulously faithful to occult truths and in his own words he does, indeed, "hold the mirror up to nature."

DREAMS

The dreams in *Richard III, Julius Caesar* and *The Winter's Tale* could be better discussed there than apart from those plays, but there are other dramas in which dreams are the only thing of special interest to the student of the occult. This is true of *Pericles, Prince of Tyre.*

It will be remembered that Pericles married Thaisa, the beautiful daughter of King Simonides; that their daughter, Marina, was born at sea; that Thaisa, supposed to be dead, was buried from the ship; that the casket was washed ashore and that she was revived and took refuge in the temple of Diana at Ephesus. The baby, Marina, was left by Pericles with Cleon and Dionyza where she grew to young womanhood; but Dionyza plotted her death and thought that it had been accomplished. A monument to Marina was erected and shown to Pericles when at last he found it possible to return for his daughter. The double loss of wife and daughter brought him close to death. When the governor of Mitylene boards the ship, Scene I, Act V, and makes inquiry about it, Helicanus replies:

                    Sir,
          Our vessel is of Tyre, in it the king;
          A man who for this three months hath not spoken
          To any one, nor taken sustenance
          But to prorogue his grief.

Lysimachus:
          Upon what ground is his distemperature?

Helicanus:
          'Twould be too tedious to repeat;
          But the main grief springs from the loss
          Of a beloved daughter and a wife.

Lysimachus:
          May we not see him?

Helicanus:
          You may;
          But bootless is your sight: he will not speak
          To any.

Lysimachus:
          Yet let me obtain my wish.

Helicanus:
          Behold him. [*Pericles discovered.*] This was a
              goodly person,
          Till the disaster that, one mortal night,
          Drove him to this.

Lysimachus:
          Sir king, all hail! the gods preserve you!
          Hail, royal sir!

Helicanus:
          It is in vain; he will not speak to you.

It was in the reaction from the great emotion
of discovering Marina alive that Pericles fell
asleep and dreamed—a dream that led him to
also discover his lost wife. It is well understood
by students of the dream state of consciousness
that the dramatizations of the ego are sometimes
brought through into the waking state and that

this is much more likely to occur when the physical body is unusually sensitive on account of illness or a condition of high nerve tension.*

Pericles:
> Most heavenly music:
> It nips me unto list'ning, and thick slumber
> Hangs upon mine eyes; let me rest.   [*Sleeps.*

Lysimachus:
> A pillow for his head.
> So, leave him all. Well, my companion friends,
> If this but answer to my just belief,
> I'll well remember you.
>   [*Exeunt all but Pericles.*
>   *Diana appears to Pericles as in a vision.*

Diana:
> My temple stands in Ephesus; hie thee thither,
> And do upon mine altar sacrifice.
> There, when my maiden priests are met together,
> Before the people all,
> Reveal how thou at sea didst lose thy wife;
> To mourn thy crosses, with thy daughter's, call
> And give them repetition to the life.
> Perform my bidding, or thou liv'st in woe;
> Do it, and happy; by my silver bow!
> Awake, and tell thy dream!   [*Disappears.*

Pericles:
> Celestial Dian, goddess argentine,
> I will obey thee! Helicanus!
>   *Enter Helicanus, Lysimachus, and Marina.*

Helicanus:
>   Sir?

Pericles:
> My purpose was for Tarsus, there to strike
> The inhospitable Cleon but I am

---

*See *Dreams,* Leadbeater; *Dreams and Premonitions,* Rogers.

> For other service first: toward Ephesus
> Turn our blown sails; eftsoons I'll tell thee why.

The next scene carries us to the temple of Diana, at Ephesus, where Thaisa is standing near the altar as high priestess, when Pericles and his train enter and we have the sequel of the dream:

Pericles:
> Hail, Dian! to perform thy just command,
> I here confess myself the King of Tyre;
> Who, frighted from my country, did wed
> At Pentapolis the fair Thaisa.
> At sea in childbed died she, but brought forth
> A maid-child call'd Marina; who, O goddess!
> Wears yet thy silver livery. She at Tarsus
> Was nurs'd with Cleon, whom at fourteen years
> He sought to murder; but her better stars
> Brought her to Mitylene, 'gainst whose shore
> Riding, her fortunes brought the maid aboard us,
> Where, by her own most clear remembrance, she
> Made known herself my daughter.

Thaisa:
>   Voice and favour!
> You are, you are—O royal Pericles!—
>   *[She faints.*

Pericles:
> What means the nun? she dies! help, gentlemen!

Cerimon:
> Noble sir,
> If you have told Diana's altar true,
> This is your wife.

Pericles:
> Reverend appearer, no;
> I threw her o'erboard with these very arms.

Cerimon:
> Upon this coast, I warrant you.

Pericles:

'Tis most certain.

Cerimon:

Look to the lady. O! she's but o'erjoy'd.
Early in blustering morn this lady was
Thrown upon this shore. I op'd the coffin,
Found there rich jewels; recover'd her, and plac'd
her
Here in Diana's temple.

Pericles:

May we see them?

Cerimon:

Great sir, they shall be brought you to my house.
Whither I invite you. Look! Thaisa is
Recovered.

Thaisa:

O! let me look!
If he be none of mine, my sanctity
Will to my sense bend no licentious ear,
But curb it, spite of seeing, O! my lord,
Are you not Pericles? Like him you speak,
Like him you are. Did you not name a tempest,
A birth, and death?

Pericles:

The voice of dead Thaisa!

Thaisa:

That Thaisa am I, supposed dead
And drown'd.

Pericles:

Immortal Dian!

Thaisa:

Now I know you better.
When we with tears parted Pentapolis,
The king my father gave you such a ring.

[*Shows a ring.*

Pericles:

This, this: no more, you gods! your present kind-
ness
Makes my past miseries sport: you shall do well,
That on the touching of her lips I may

> Melt and no more be seen. O! come, be buried
> A second time within these arms.

The Duke of Gloucester, Lord Protector of the realm during the minority of the king, has a symbolical dream which accurately forecasts the future. His wife, the duchess, secretly covets the throne and finally communicates her thought to the duke in Scene II of Act I, *Second Part of King Henry VI.* This leads him to mention his "troublous dream."

Duchess:
> Why droops my lord, like over-ripen'd corn
> Hanging the head at Ceres' plenteous load?
> Why doth the great Duke Humphrey knit his
>   brows,
> As frowning at the favours of the world?
> Why are thine eyes fix'd to the sullen earth,
> Gazing on that which seems to dim thy sight?
> What seest thou there? King Henry's diadem
> Enchas'd with all the honours of the world?
> If so, gaze on, and grovel on thy face,
> Until thy head be circled with the same.
> Put forth thy hand, reach at the glorious gold;
> What! is't too short? I'll lengthen it with mine;
> And having both together heav'd it up,
> We'll both together lift our heads to heaven,
> And never more abase our sight so low
> As to vouchsafe one glance unto the ground.

Gloucester:
> O Nell, sweet Nell, if thou dost love thy lord,
> Banish the canker of ambitious thoughts:
> And may that thought, when I imagine ill
> Against my king and nephew, virtuous Henry,
> Be my last breathing in this mortal world!

My troublous dream this night doth make me
sad.
Duchess:
What dream'd my lord? tell me, and I'll requite
it
With sweet rehearsal of my morning's dream.
Gloucester:
Methought this staff, mine office badge in court,
Was broke in twain; by whom I have forgot,
But, as I think, it was by the cardinal;
And on the pieces of the broken wand
Were plac'd the heads of Edmund Duke of
Somerset,
And William De la Pole, first Duke of Suffolk.
This was my dream: what it doth bode, God
knows.

Meantime better rivalry is growing between
the duchess and the young queen. In Scene III,
Act I, the latter says to Suffolk:

Queen Margaret:
Not all these lords do vex me half so much
As that proud dame, the Lord Protector's wife:
She sweeps it through the court with troops of
ladies,
More like an empress than Duke Humphrey's
wife.
Strangers in court do take her for the queen:
She bears a duke's revenues on her back,
And in her heart she scorns our poverty.
Shall I not live to be aveng'd on her?
Contemptuous base-born callot as she is,
She vaunted 'mongst her minions t'other day
The very train of her worst wearing gown
Was better worth than all my father's lands,
Till Suffolk gave two dukedoms for his daughter.

Suffolk, however, has laid a deep plot to

subtly use the ambition of the duchess for her own downfall and later to bring ruin to the honest Duke of Gloucester, and he replies to the queen:

> Madam, myself have lim'd a bush for her,
> And plac'd a quire of such enticing birds
> That she will light to listen to the lays,
> And never mount to trouble you again.
> So, let her rest: and, madam, list to me;
> For I am bold to counsel you in this.
> Although we fancy not the cardinal,
> Yet must we join with him and with the lords
> Till we have brought Duke Humphrey in disgrace.

As soon as the duchess has been trapped through her own foolish ambitions the plotters, now joined by the Cardinal, Duke of Somerset and others, boldly moved in the matter of falsely accusing the Duke of Gloucester of treason. In Scene I, Act III, the duke enters and salutes the king.

Gloucester:
> All happiness unto my lord the king!
> Pardon, my liege, that I have stay'd so long.

Suffolk:
> Nay, Gloucester, know that thou art come too soon,
> Unless thou wert more loyal than thou art:
> I do arrest thee of high treason here.

Gloucester:
> Well, Suffolk's duke, thou shalt not see me blush,
> Nor change my countenance for this arrest:
> A heart unspotted is not easily daunted.

The purest spring is not so free from mud
As I am clear from treason to my sovereign.
Who can accuse me? wherein am I guilty?

Now that the accusation is made the plotters
discuss the next step. When the king has left
the room and Gloucester has departed, under ar-
rest, the queen says:

This Gloucester should be quickly rid the world,
To rid us from the fear we have of him.
Cardinal:
That he should die is worthy policy;
And yet we want a colour for his death.
'Tis meet he be condemn'd by course of law.
Suffolk:
But in my mind that were no policy:
The king will labour still to save his life;
The commons haply rise to save his life;
And yet we have but trivial argument,
More than mistrust, that shows him worthy death.
York:
So that, by this, you would not have him die.
Suffolk:
Ah! York, no man alive so fain as I.
York:
'Tis York that hath more reason for his death.
But my Lord Cardinal, and you, my Lord of
Suffolk,
Say as you think, and speak it from your souls,
Were't not all one an empty eagle were set
To guard the chicken from a hungry kite,
As place Duke Humphrey for the king's pro-
tector?
Queen Margaret:
So the poor chicken should be sure of death.
Suffolk:
Madam, 'tis true: and were't not madness, then,
To make the fox surveyor of the fold?

> Who, being accus'd a crafty murderer,
> His guilt should be but idly posted over
> Because his purpose is not executed.
> No; let him die, in that he is a fox,
> By nature prov'd an enemy to the flock,
> Before his chaps be stain'd with crimson blood,
> As Humphrey, prov'd by reasons, to my liege,
> And do not stand on quillets how to slay him:
> Be it by gins, by snares, by subtilty,
> Sleeping or waking, 'tis no matter how,
> So he be dead; for that is good deceit
> Which mates him first that first intends deceit.

Queen Margaret:
> Thrice noble Suffolk, 'tis resolutely spoke.

Suffolk:
> Not resolute, except so much were done,
> For things were often spoke and seldom meant;
> But, that my heart accordeth with my tongue,
> Seeing the deed is meritorious,
> And to preserve my sovereign from his foe,
> Say but the word and I will be his priest.

Cardinal:
> But I would have him dead, my Lord of Suffolk,
> Ere you can take due orders for a priest:
> Say you consent and censure well the deed,
> And I'll provide his executioner;
> I tender so the safety of my liege.

Suffolk:
> Here is my hand, the deed is worthy doing.

Queen Margaret:
> And so say I.

York:
> And I: and now we three have spoke it,
> It skills not greatly who impugns our doom.

They are interrupted by the messenger with news of rebellion. After that Suffolk brings the conversation back to the Duke of Gloucester and the Cardinal says:

No more of him; for I will deal with him
That henceforth he shall trouble us no more.
And so break off; the day is almost spent.
Lord Suffolk, you and I must talk of that event.

What came of their conference is clear in
Scene II, Act III.

First Murderer:
Run to my Lord of Suffolk; let him know
We have dispatch'd the duke, as he commanded.
Second Murderer:
O! that it were to do. What have we done?
Didst ever hear a man so penitent?
Enter Suffolk.
First Murderer:
Here comes my lord.
Suffolk:
Now, sirs, have you dispatch'd this thing?
First Murderer:
Ay, my good lord, he's dead.
Suffolk:
Why, that's well said. Go, get you to my house;
I will reward you for this venturous deed.

The whole of the plot had now worked out as
planned but the chief conspirators did not live
long afterward. Almost immediately Suffolk fell
into disfavor with the king and he banished him,
and in attempting to travel in disguise he was
captured by Whitmore, and beheaded as related
under "Ceremonial Magic." The fate of the
Cardinal is told in Scene II and Scene III of Act
III.

Queen Margaret:
Whither goes Vaux so fast? what news, I prithee?

Vaux:
> To signify unto his majesty
> That Cardinal Beaufort is at point of death;
> For suddenly a grievous sickness took him,
> That makes him gasp and stare, and catch the air,
> Blaspheming God, and cursing men on earth.
> Sometimes he talks as if Duke Humphrey's ghost
> Were by his side; sometimes he calls the king,
> And whispers to his pillow, as to him,
> The secrets of his overcharged soul:
> And I am sent to tell his majesty
> That even now he cries aloud for him.

Scene III is the Cardinal's bed chamber where just before his death, enter the king, Salisbury and Warwick.

King Henry:
> How fares my lord? speak, Beaufort, to thy
>   sovereign.

Cardinal:
> If thou be'st death, I'll give thee England's
>   treasure,
> Enough to purchase such another island,
> So thou wilt let me live, and feel no pain.

King Henry:
> Ah! what a sign it is of evil life
> Where death's approach is seen so terrible.

Warwick:
> Beaufort, it is thy sov'reign speaks to thee.

Cardinal:
> Bring me unto my trial when you will.
> Died he not in his bed? where should he die?
> Can I make men live whe'r they will or not?
> O! torture me no more, I will confess.
> Alive again? then show me where he is:
> I'll give a thousand pound to look upon him.
> He hath no eyes, the dust hath blinded them.
> Comb down his hair; look! look! it stands upright

Like lime-twigs set to catch my winged soul.
Give me some drink; and bid the apothecary
Bring the strong poison that I bought of him.

Somerset, who had briefly enjoyed the place
of influence close to the king left vacant by the
banishment of Suffolk, later met a violent death
"underneath an alehouse paltry sign" as described under the caption "Ceremonial Magic."

Romeo had a dream which the student of after
death conditions would probably say was, with
its mingled emotions of death and triumph, a
combination of forecast of the coming tragedy
and memory of astral consciousness. In Scene
I, Act V, the text runs:

Romeo:
If I may trust the flattering truth of sleep,
My dreams presage some joyful news at hand:
My bosom's lord sits lightly in his throne;
And all this day an unaccustom'd spirit
Lifts me above the ground with cheerful thoughts.
I dreamt my lady came and found me dead;—
Strange dream, that gives a dead man leave to
think—
And breath'd such life with kisses in my lips,
That I reviv'd, and was an emperor.
Ah me! how sweet is love itself possess'd,
When but love's shadows are so rich in joy!

Balthasar, after going with Romeo to the
tomb, is ordered to go away but instead of doing
so he retreats to another part of the grounds

and, while lying under a tree, falls asleep. Paris comes, fights with Romeo, and is killed. When Balthasar awakens he says:

> As I did sleep under this yew-tree here,
> I dreamt my master and another fought,
> And that my master slew him.

When Roderigo and Iago in Scene I, Act I, *Othello*, arouse Brabantio in the night and give him the unwelcome news that Desdemona and Othello are married, he exclaims:

> This accident is not unlike my dream.

The dream, however, is not related.

PREMONITIONS

There are a number of instances of premonitions scattered through various plays. One of these arises from the dishonorable act of Prince John of Lancaster in directing the opposing army, led by dissatisfied noblemen, into disbanding on pretense that their wrongs would be righted and then treacherously seizing the generals, after, upon his sacred promise, their forces had been disbanded. After Lancaster's messenger, Westmoreland, had persuaded Lord Mowbray, Lord Hastings and the Archbishop of York that peace and justice could be secured without battle and they had ridden forward to parley with the prince, we have the following in Scene II, Act IV, *Second Part of King Henry IV*:

Lancaster:

> You are well encounter'd here, my cousin Mowbray:
> Good day to you, gentle lord archbishop;
> And so to you, Lord Hastings, and to all.
> My Lord of York, it better show'd with you,
> When that your flock, assembled by the bell,
> Encircled you to hear with reverence
> Your exposition on the holy text
> Than now to see you here an iron man,
> Cheering a rout of rebels with your drum,

Turning the word to sword and life to death.
That man that sits within a monarch's heart
And ripens in the sunshine of his favour,
Would he abuse the countenance of the king,
Alack! what mischief might he set abroach
In shadow of such greatness. With you, lord
    bishop,
It is even so. Who hath not heard it spoken
How deep you were within the books of God?
To us, the speaker in his parliament;
To us the imagin'd voice of God himself;
The very opener and intelligencer
Between the grace, the sanctities of heaven,
And our dull workings. O! who shall believe
But you misuse the reverence of your place,
Employ the countenance and grace of heaven,
As a false favourite doth his prince's name,
In deed dishonourable? You have taken up,
Under the counterfeited zeal of God,
The subjects of his substitute, my father;
And both against the peace of heaven and him
Have here upswarm'd them.

Archbishop:
                    Good my Lord of Lancaster,
I am not here against your father's peace;
But, as I told my Lord of Westmoreland,
The time misorder'd doth, in common sense,
Crowd us and crush us to this monstrous form,
To hold our safety up. I sent your Grace
The parcels and particulars of our grief,—
The which hath been with scorn shov'd from the
    court,—
Whereon this Hydra son of war is born;
Whose dangerous eyes may well be charm'd
    asleep
With grant of our most just and right desires,
And true obedience, of this madness cur'd,
Stoop tamely to the foot of majesty.

Mowbray:
If not, we ready are to try our fortunes
To the last man.

Hastings:
>And though we here fall down,
>We have supplies to second our attempt:
>If they miscarry, theirs shall second them;
>And so success of mischief shall be born,
>And heir from heir shall hold this quarrel up
>Whiles England shall have generation.

Lancaster:
>You are too shallow, Hastings, much too shallow,
>To sound the bottom of the after-times.

Westmoreland:
>Pleaseth your Grace, to answer them directly
>How far forth you do like their articles.

Lancaster:
>I like them all, and do allow them well;
>And swear here, by the honour of my blood,
>My father's purposes have been mistook,
>And some about him have too lavishly
>Wrested his meaning and authority.
>My lord, these griefs shall be with speed re-
>>dress'd;
>Upon my soul, they shall. If this may please you,
>Discharge your powers unto their several coun-
>>ties,
>As we will ours: and here between the armies
>Let's drink together friendly and embrace,
>That all their eyes may bear those tokens home
>Of our restored love and amity.

Archbishop:
>I take your princely word for these redresses.

Lancaster:
>I give it you, and will maintain my word:
>And thereupon I drink unto your Grace.

Hastings [*To an officer*]:
>Go, captain, and deliver to the army
>This news of peace: let them have pay, and part:
>I know it will well please them: hie thee, captain.
>>>>[*Exit Officer.*

Archbishop:
>To you, my noble Lord of Westmoreland.

Westmoreland:
    I pledge your Grace: and, if you knew what pains
    I have bestow'd to breed this present peace,
    You would drink freely; but my love to you
    Shall show itself more openly hereafter.

Archbishop:
    I do not doubt you.

Westmoreland:
                I am glad of it.
    Health to my lord and gentle cousin, Mowbray.

Mowbray:
    You wish me health in very happy season;
    For I am, on the sudden, something ill.

Archbishop:
    Against ill chances men are ever merry,
    But heaviness foreruns the good event.

Westmoreland:
    Therefore be merry, coz; since sudden sorrow
    Serves to say thus, Some good thing comes to-
        morrow.

Archbishop:
    Believe me, I am passing light in spirit.

Mowbray:
    So much the worse if your own rule be true.
                    [Shouts within.

Lancaster:
    The word of peace is render'd: hark, how they
        shout!

Mowbray:
    This had been cheerful, after victory.

Archbishop:
    A peace is of the nature of a conquest;
    For then both parties nobly are subdu'd,
    And neither party loser.

Lancaster:
               Go, my lord,
    And let our army be discharged too.
                [Exit Westmoreland.
    And, good my lord, so please you, let our trains
    March by us, that we may peruse the men
    We should have cop'd withal.

Archbishop:
> Go, good Lord Hastings,
> And, ere they be dismiss'd, let them march by.
> > *[Exit Hastings.*

Lancaster:
> I trust, lords, we shall lie to-night together.
> > *Re-enter Westmoreland.*
> Now, cousin, wherefore stands our army still?

Westmoreland:
> The leaders, having charge from you to stand,
> Will not go off until they hear you speak.

Lancaster:
> They know their duties.
> > *Re-enter Hastings.*

Hastings:
> My lord, our army is dispers'd already;
> Like youthful steers unyok'd, they take their
> > courses
> East, west, north, south; or, like a school broke
> > up,
> Each hurries toward his home and sporting place.

Westmoreland:
> Good tidings, my Lord Hastings; for the which
> I do arrest thee, traitor, of high treason:
> And you, lord archbishop, and you, Lord Mow-
> > bray,
> Of capital treason I attach you both.

Mowbray:
> Is this proceeding just and honourable?

Westmoreland:
> Is your assembly so?

Archbishop:
> Will you thus break your faith?

Lancaster:
> > I pawn'd thee none.
> I promis'd you redress of these same grievances
> Whereof you did complain; which, by mine
> > honour,
> I will perform with a most Christian care.
> But for you, rebels, look to taste the due

> Meet for rebellion and such acts as yours.
> Most shallowly did you these arms commence,
> Fondly brought here and foolishly sent hence.
> Strike up your drums! pursue the scatter'd stray:
> God, and not we, hath safely fought to-day.
> Some guard these traitors to the block of death;
> Treason's true bed, and yielder up of breath.

At the moment that Mowbray became "on a sudden, something ill," there was absolutely nothing on the surface to indicate the very near approach of death. There was every reason to believe that the prince desired only to avoid bloodshed and that his heart was in his declaration,

> —and here between the armies
> Let's drink together friendly and embrace,
> That all their eyes may bear these tokens home
> Of our restored love and amity.

Mowbray, when discussing the matter with Westmoreland before meeting the prince, says:

> There is a thing within my bosom tells me
> That no conditions of our peace can stand.

Hastings and the Archbishop, however, argued to the contrary and Mowbray finally yielded.

In *Titus Andronicus*, it will be remembered that Aaron, the most diabolical of all the villains in the various Shakespeare plays, lays a deep plot that, among its other devilish devices, leads to the execution of Quintus and Martius. In

order to fasten upon them the guilt of Deme-
trius and Chiron, who had just killed the emperor's brother and thrown his body into a pit,
Aaron, after hiding the bag of gold and prepar-
ing other incriminating evidence, brings the two
brothers to the spot where Martius falls into the
pit in which the body of the emperor's brother
has been thrown. Immediately after that
Quintus is seized with an unaccountable fear. In
Scene III, Act II, the text runs thus:

Aaron:
      Come on, my lords, the better foot before:
      Straight will I bring you to the loathsome pit
      Where I espied the panther fast asleep.
Quintus:
      My sight is very dull, whate'er it bodes.
Martius:
      And mine, I promise you: were't not for shame,
      Well could I leave our sport to sleep awhile.
                        [*Falls into the pit.*
Quintus:
      What! art thou fall'n? What subtle hole is this,
      Whose mouth is cover'd with rude-growing briers,
      Upon whose leaves are drops of new-shed blood
      As fresh as morning's dew distill'd on flowers?
      A very fatal place it seems to me.
      Speak, brother, hast thou hurt thee with the fall?
Martius:
      O brother! with the dismall'st object hurt
      That ever eye with sight made heart lament.
Aaron [*Aside*]:
      Now will I fetch the king to find them here,
      That he thereby may give a likely guess
      How these were they that made away his brother.
                              [*Exit.*

Martius:
>   Why dost not comfort me, and help me out
>   From this unhallow'd and blood-stained hole?

Quintus:
>   I am surprised with an uncouth fear;
>   A chilling sweat o'erruns my trembling joints:
>   My heart suspects more than mine eye can see.

As with Mowbray it was apparently a groundless but a mighty fear. Although a warrior accustomed to bloody combat Quintus was so unnerved that he could not assist his brother from the pit and exclaims:

>   O! tell me how it is; for ne'er till now
>   Was I a child, to fear I know not what.

The next appearance of the innocent brothers is when they are taken, bound, to the place of execution.

Both Romeo and Juliet have presentiments of the coming tragedy and Romeo's comes very early in the drama. When he and his companions are masking in the street, in Scene IV of Act I, prior to going into Capulet's house, the conversation is between Mercutio and Romeo.

Romeo:
>   Peace, peace! Mercutio, peace!
>   Thou talk'st of nothing.

Mercutio:
>   True, I talk of dreams,
>   Which are the children of an idle brain,
>   Begot of nothing but vain fantasy;
>   Which is as thin of substance as the air,

And more inconstant than the wind, who woos
Even now the frozen bosom of the north,
And, being anger'd, puffs away from thence,
Turning his face to the dew-dropping south.
Benvolio:
This wind you talk of blows us from ourselves;
Supper is done, and we shall come too late.
Romeo:
I fear too early; for my mind misgives
Some consequence yet hanging in the stars
Shall bitterly begin his fearful date
With this night's revels, and expire the term
Of a despised life clos'd in my breast
By some vile forfeit of untimely death.
But he, that hath the steerage of my course,
Direct my sail! On, lusty gentlemen.

Juliet's premonition comes when in Scene V,
Act III, Romeo takes his leave.

Juliet:
O! think'st thou we shall ever meet again?
Romeo:
I doubt it not; and all these woes shall serve
For sweet discourses in our time to come.
Juliet:
O God! I have an ill-divining soul:
Methinks I see thee, now thou art so low,
As one dead in the bottom of a tomb:
Either my eyesight fails, or thou look'st pale.

When Juliet sees her mother for the last time
(Scene III, Act IV) she says:

Farewell! God knows when we shall meet again.
I have a faint cold fear thrills through my veins,
That almost freezes up the heat of life:

Portia, wife of Brutus, had a haunting impression of impending tragedy. In Scene IV, Act II, of *Julius Caesar* she says to her servant boy Lucius:

> Yes, bring me word, boy, if thy lord look well,
> For he went sickly forth; and take good note
> What Caesar doth, what suitors press to him.
> Hark, boy! what noise is that?

Lucius:
> I hear none, madam.

Portia:
> Prithee, listen well:
> I heard a bustling rumour, like a fray,
> And the wind brings it from the Capitol.

Lucius:
> Sooth, madam, I hear nothing.

This was shortly before Caesar arrived at the capitol. The fray soon afterward became a reality. Portia knows nothing whatever of the conspirators' plans; yet she intuitively gets exactly the general situation even to the part that "Brutus hath a suit that Caesar will not grant." In the same scene she says:

> I must go in. Ay me! how weak a thing
> The heart of woman is. O Brutus!
> The heavens speed thee in thine enterprise.
> Sure, the boy heard me: Brutus hath a suit
> That Caesar will not grant. O! I grow faint.

CONCLUSION

In all the occultism in the Shakespeare plays one fact stands out clear and unquestionable; *it is always presented as the truth.* The dreams, visions and prophecies are never the fantastic products of disordered brains, but always they forecast the future faithfully. It is nowhere intimated that all dreams are of that kind, but that there is a type of dream with that possibility is repeatedly set forth. In every particular case all the varied occultism is treated with dignity and sincerity.

One thing that seems to have puzzled the critics of these matchless plays is their consistency. Not crediting the invisible world as a fact in nature they have marveled that the dramatist unites the visible and the invisible in so complete and consistent a whole. One puzzled writer exclaims, "by making what is absolutely unnatural thoroughly natural and consistent he has accomplished the impossible!"

Such consistency can be expressed only by one who deals with the truth. If a clever witness in court has, for personal reasons, concocted a story that is false, the most ordinary lawyer will be able to expose his untruthfulness, point out his contradictions and break down his testimony; but if the stupidest of witnesses is telling the truth, and basing his narrative on facts, all the cross-questioning, directed by the highest skill, can never shake his testimony. Consistency is merely loyalty to the truth, and when the critics say that by making what is absolutely unnatural thoroughly natural and consistent the great author has accomplished the impossible, they have given the highest possible testimony in support of the hypothesis that he was not dealing with imagination at all but with a great region of nature that is unknown to physical senses. This is a simple and most reasonable explanation of the thing that puzzles them. Hazlett contents himself by calling it genius and says that "there can be little doubt that Shakespeare was the most universal genius that ever lived"; and again he remarks that he had "the same insight into the world of imagination that he had into the world of reality." But it is no explanation of a mystery to say that genius produced it. It *is* an explanation to show that it ceases to be a mystery when viewed in the light of the scientific facts and philosophical principles that establish the existence of a superphysical world inhabited by various orders of beings. The fact that in this most dignified literature, which is almost universally admitted to show profound wisdom and a marvelous comprehension of human nature, we have corroboration of the researches of both psychical and physical scientists is assuredly one that may not be lightly dismissed.

It is amusing to see how different people are struck with the poet's exact technical knowledge on subjects with which they happen to be familiar and how they try to account for it, ignoring the fact that he is quite as much at home with all the other subjects. Lord Mulgrave, who is mentioned as a distinguished naval officer, says that the first scene in *The Tempest* "is a very striking instance of Shakespeare's knowledge in a professional science, the most difficult to obtain without the help of experience. He must have acquired it by conversation with some of the most skillful seamen of that time." If the poet-dramatist acquired his marvelous fund of information by consulting experts on each subject it would puzzle the critics more to understand how he had time for anything else than to satisfactorily account for his genius.

But if we accept the most probable explanation
—that he was an occultist to whom cause and
effect in the two worlds lay open—the solution
of all the puzzles in his literary work becomes
simple.

Those who cannot see that the occultism which
permeates such of the Shakespeare plays as it
naturally belongs to, is there because it is as
legitimate a part of them as trees and grass are
part of a landscape, have, so far as I know,
offered no other explanation than that "the great
dramatist was making a concession to the superstition of his times." Such an explanation is
wholly inadequate for a number of reasons. In
the first place if it were merely a concession to
the ignorant there would be no reason for it being the notable thing it is in some of the plays.
It would be incidental, not vital. We would expect it to be in the form of allusions here and
there, as a politician throws out to his audience
complimentary and pleasing remarks that have
no bearing on his arguments and no part in his
purpose. But why should there be a "concession" at all? Why was it necessary? Why was
it more necessary in the Shakespeare plays than
in any others of that age? Why didn't Jonson
and other successful dramatists of the same age

have to make the same concession? In *The Alchemist* Jonson makes a savage attack upon astrology. He represents its practitioners as barefaced frauds of the most contemptible type and their patrons as credulous fools; and that undoubtedly pleased the majority then as it would now.

The Shakespeare plays were not written to cater to the passions of the times. With their inherent strength and beauty they can win their way against the prejudices of any age. Moreover, if it had been necessary for a play to have some "superstition" in it, in order to succeed, why was it necessary in some of these plays and not in others? If it was necessary for the success of *A Midsummer-Night's Dream* why was it not also necessary for *As You Like It?* If it was essential to the success of *Hamlet* and *Macbeth* why not also for *Othello* or *The Merchant of Venice?* The simple truth is that the occultism appears only where it naturally belongs and for the purpose of teaching the lesson that is being presented.

But there are other reasons for rejecting the theory that the great dramatist was making a concession to the ignorance of his times. The plays do not belong exclusively to that age and bear most convincing internal evidence that they were not written for that time any more than for this time or for the future generations. Certainly nobody better than the author himself understood that. It was more than two centuries before this greatest literary achievement of the modern world came to be really appreciated in fair degree. These plays will undoubtedly be more fully appreciated in future times than in our own, for what is their "superstition" to this generation will be their science to the next. They belong to all ages because they deal with the fundamentals of nature and will be read with profit as long as men seek to analyze human motives and study the evolution of the race.

Perhaps the most cogent answer of all to the inadequate explanation that the great poet-dramatist was making "a concession to the superstition of his times" is that such a course would have been a prostitution of his genius inconsistent with the character of his work. His greatness as a teacher is beyond all question; and nothing could be more reprehensible than for one who is far beyond others in intelligence to fasten upon the people wrong beliefs. To lend his pen to any such base purpose would be evidence of a moral weakness and cowardice that could not have belonged to the character of the man who produced these plays, for their moral strength and grandeur is more striking than even their intellectual power. No man capable of that ignoble course could possibly have created such characters as Prospero and Cordelia, or have given us the lofty ideals we find in such plays as *The Tempest* and in *Romeo and Juliet*. The truth is that instead of degrading his work to please the popular conception of his times he took precisely the opposite course; and in an age when lust, cruelty and revenge were exceedingly popular he exalted and glorified purity, pity and forgiveness.